HEALING the ORPHANED HEART

Renewal for the Misunderstood, the Abused, and the Abandoned

D1015307

HEALING the ORPHANED HEART

Renewal for the Misunderstood, the Abused, and the Abandoned

by
Casey Treat

Harrison House
Tulsa, Oklahoma

07 06 05 04 03   10 9 8 7 6 5 4 3 2 1

Healing the Orphaned Heart—
Renewal for the Misunderstood, the Abused, and the Abandoned
ISBN 1-57794-451-8
Copyright © 2003 by Casey Treat
Christian Faith International
P. O. Box 98800
Seattle, WA 98198

Published by Harrison House, Inc.
P. O. Box 35035
Tulsa, OK 74153

Contents

Pastors' Comments

As a pastor, I have often dealt with people who could never seem to connect or give or receive love. It wasn't until I heard Pastor Treat talk about people having an orphan's heart that I fully understood the problem. Casey not only reveals the problem, he gives real applicable answers. I hope every believer reads this book. It will help them and empower them to help others.

Pastor Charles Nieman
Abundant Living Faith Center
El Paso, Texas

Proverbs 4:23—"Keep your heart with all diligence, for out of it spring the issues of life." It's true—we can trace every problem in our life back to a heart issue. Get a good heart and obtain a great life!

In this great book, *Overcoming the Orphan's Heart,* Casey reveals the symptoms of an orphan's heart, and then masterfully shows us how with God's help, plus our choices, we can have a whole, clean and perfect heart.

Pastor Rick Godwin
Eagle's Nest Christian Fellowship
San Antonio, Texas

Casey Treat has been one of the most consistent and anointed ministers of the Gospel that I have had the pleasure to be close to over the past fifteen years.

He has been a great blessing to the body of Christ around the world, and in particular, to us in Africa.

This teaching has been a wonderful inspiration and has changed many people's lives, and I believe it will do the same for you. I highly recommend this book.

Pastor Ray McCauley
Rhema Ministries
South Africa

1

The Heart Is the Inner Man—Spirit and Soul

When Jesus said, "I will not leave you orphans," He was speaking to men who had grown up with both parents, were working in their family's businesses, and were preparing for ministry. Why did He refer to His disciples as orphans? He was not speaking of their natural families or circumstances.

Jesus saw the condition of their hearts—their need for a new relationship with their heavenly Father and for healing of hurts, insecurities, and other things that would limit their lives. Jesus was beginning the process of building a new treasure into their hearts, for He knew the Word and work of God would have to flow out of their hearts. Being born again was only the first step in living the abundant life that Jesus came to give them. He was reaching for those things within them that brought the limitations and defensiveness and hindered them from receiving all He had for them.

You and I are no different from disciples two thousand years ago. We all need to overcome the things in our heart that come from parents who didn't know God's Word or public schools that teach secular humanism or circumstances that were orchestrated by the enemy to hurt and destroy us.

The orphan's heart is one of hurts and insecurities that limit and eventually control our lives. If we receive healing and renewal from the Lord, the orphan's heart will never slow us down. But if we do not, the orphan's heart will pull us down to defeat and despair.

The major factor in the condition of your heart is how you were raised and particularly the example set by your parents or those who filled the role of Mom and Dad. They raised you with security or insecurity, confidence or fear, discipline or rebellion. Our earthly "father and mother" have more impact on us than we may want to admit. In today's world, so many of our parents are struggling with their divorce, financial pressures, loneliness, and other crises that they are not able to give to their children the whole heart they need. It's not that they don't want to, but they are not equipped to meet the needs of their children. Consequently, many children grow up with hearts that lack basic ingredients for success in life.

My Three Fathers

I've had three earthly fathers in my life. The first was William Treat, a man raised on a farm in Nebraska, who fought for America in Korea, worked as a carpenter after his military service, and wanted to talk to his roping horse more than anyone else. My dad was a good man who went to work every day, paid his bills, and was nice to people. When I was going through drug problems and his marriage was breaking up, he tried to fix them both. He did his best, but it didn't work. He had no skills at building relationships and no understanding of the thoughts and feelings that his wife—my mother—

or I had. He died at a relatively young age, still going to work every day and talking to his horses every night.

My second father was Julius Young. We met when I entered the Washington Drug Rehabilitation Center in 1974. Julius was a fifty-four-year-old black man who had been raised in Washington D.C. and spent twenty-four years of his life in prison. He was a heroin addict, drug dealer, and hustler. He prayed to God while in prison that He might do something with his life, and God was listening. After eighteen years and no parole in sight, Julius was miraculously released. He was soon born again and started the Washington Drug Rehabilitation Center. Less than one year later, I walked through the front door of the program and joined the other twenty-five or so residents. We were a "family" and sought the same help and healing. Most of those who entered the program didn't stay long, but I did. Julius became my mentor, friend, big brother, and spiritual father. He believed in me and saw God's hand upon my life. He challenged me to grow and not accept less than God's best. He was the first elder at Christian Faith Center when we started in 1980, and he died in 1985. Julius was a good father.

My third father is Frederick K.C. Price. Though I have never lived in his house, he has spoken more truth into my life over the past twenty years than any other man. I first saw Pastor Price on television, and then at seminars. Wendy and I spent a week at Crenshaw Christian Center in 1980, and he and Betty have been our pastors and spiritual parents ever since.

Pastor Price has put uncompromising principles from God's Word in my heart, he has raised my vision and goals to a higher realm, and he has set a course for a long, prosperous, abundant life that I believe I will be able to fulfill.

I only see Pastor Price once in a while on a personal level, but through television, books, and tapes, I receive his support and follow his example. I know he has many spiritual children throughout the world, but I have always felt like a special red-haired son to him. He and Betty have helped Wendy and me in so many ways through the years. Most of the time they didn't even know how much they did for us. Their example in good times and bad, their love and support, and their commitment to the Lord have always been there. Pastor Price is a good father.

The results of the first nineteen years of my life show the condition of my heart at that time. I was bringing forth addictions, sin, and shame because of the choices and relationships I put myself into. After coming to the Lord, I began to renew my mind and the treasure in my heart, and the results of my life began to show it. Through a relationship with my heavenly Father and mentoring from new mentors on earth, I began to live life on a whole new level.

Many Christians today are not enjoying abundant life. They struggle with poverty, sickness, depression...all things that are normal to people who do not know the Lord. The reason this is true is because of the condition of their hearts. Not that they're in sin, but they have not received the renewal necessary to bring forth abundant life on earth. We try to explain these negative things by saying they're God's will or the attack of Satan, but the truth is, we need to make some changes. Remember, Jesus told us to pray for His will to be done on earth, not when we get to heaven.

Through the Word of God and twenty-five years of renewing my orphan's heart, I have learned the steps to change the things that held me back from moving into my promised land. Don't settle for surviving in the wilderness; go for the abundant life in the land that flows with milk and honey. It's yours. It's God's will for you. As we walk together through the chapters of this book, you will experience change and renewal that will empower you to bring forth that treasure that the Lord has put in your heart, and enter the blessed life that He came to give you.

Spirit, Soul, or Body—
Where's the Problem?

When facing the problems of life, there are several schools of thought as to how we can change and overcome. Some believe it is all about the physical. They are convinced that our DNA is established at conception and that in our body are the controlling factors of our life. Weight problems, attitudes, personalities, addictions, even tendencies to crime are believed to be in the physical makeup of the individual. Scientists are working to adjust or control the DNA of humans to "manufacture" the perfect person.

Others believe it's in the mind. If we can be educated and trained with the right things, we will be successful and positive people. Psychiatrists and psychologists are studying diligently to find answers to the problems of human life. Drug therapies to affect the thought processes are believed to be of value in some cases. They believe if we can control the mind, we can control the life.

Even though we have come so far in understanding the physical and mental makeup of people, we still can't stop the problems of everyday life. With all our wisdom and abilities, we still cannot stop the breakdown of families, the abuse of the weak, or the hatred of racism. Why do people destroy their own lives with habits like smoking, drinking, overeating, or drugs when the knowledge to solve these problems is so readily available? Why do some destroy their relationships with their spouse, children, or friends when communication skills and relationship insights abound?

The answer is because it's not just physical or intellectual things that control our lives. It's the condition of the heart. Our inner person, made up of soul and spirit (Heb. 4:12), is deciding how we live our lives. Proverbs 4:23 says to "guard your heart for out of it spring the issues of life."

We so often want the external things in our lives to change. We want better jobs, more money, different relationships, or even a healthier body. These are all physical things and one would think they would be easy to change. Especially in free countries where opportunities abound, we can *go* where we want to go, and *do* what we want to do. Even in underprivileged circumstances, we see people who break out and live new lives, and change the physical aspects of their world.

But many people never do change and are stuck in the negative things of their world. They blame the people around them——the government, their boss, their spouse, or even the Lord——and they do not change. These are the people who must read this message; this book is for you. You can change your external physical world, but the condition of your heart is not changed by changing the things *around* you; rather it's accomplished by changing what is *in* you. As your heart is changed, you begin to bring forth new things, and external change happens. From the inside out, you can change your life.

My friend Kennedy Akinlosotu was born in Nigeria in some of the worst conditions on the earth. Poverty, crime, war, and death were a normal part of his world. Somehow Kennedy decided he wanted something different for his future, something different for his life. Eventually he came to America, the land of the free where "everyone is a millionaire," but he found that everything did not change for him. Even though he had escaped the negatives of the land he was raised in, he brought part of it with him. His heart was full of the limitations he had been raised with. That's when he realized he needed more than a new address; he needed a new heart. God was dealing with Kennedy and soon he was born again. Jesus came into his life and he began to change. He learned the new birth is only the beginning of a changed heart. He also had to renew his mind and begin to think the thoughts of God. As these things happened in his life, his heart was healed and changed. The "orphan's heart" of abandonment, hatred, hurt and pain were replaced by a whole heart full of God's Word and God's Spirit. Today, Kennedy is a prosperous businessman and a great family man. He is part of our church family, helping us to build a great church in the Pacific Northwest. What's the difference between him and many others who are born into poverty, war, and negative circumstances? Is it luck, welfare, or God's sovereignty? It is a whole heart! He overcame his broken heart and became whole on the inside; then everything on the outside changed too.

Loneliness and the Orphan's Heart

Loneliness is a major part of the orphan's heart. The need and desire for intimacy causes all of us to do things that are not always healthy. Many a young girl has had sex with her boyfriend to keep him from leaving her or because of her fear of losing him. Many a wife has allowed abuse to continue in her home because of the fear of being alone. She decided it was better to have an abusive husband than none at all.

The first step to overcoming loneliness, or the fear of it, is to have a real relationship with your heavenly

Father. Our spirit cries out for spiritual intimacy with God. No matter what we try—alcohol, drugs, sex, sports, various spiritualist cults—we will not be fulfilled. Jesus said that we must be born again to see the kingdom of God. (John 3:3-6.) This spiritual birth takes place when we commit our lives to Christ and believe He is Lord. (Rom. 10:9,10.) Now, as a Christian you have relationship with God through your spirit. The emptiness begins to leave and you have an opportunity to develop a whole heart. It will not happen automatically, but this is the birth, or the first step to wholeness. Initially, the biggest change is the loss of spiritual emptiness, separation from your Father, and loneliness. We must continue to grow and "work out our salvation" (Phil. 2:13) but now we are on our way.

The other aspect of loneliness in the orphan's heart is only changed through relationship with people. Jesus said we must love God and love each other. Both are necessary for a whole heart. Relationships are hard and often painful but they also hold the key for fulfillment in life. No one can succeed as an island, and he who isolates himself is not wise. (Prov. 18:1.) We are all parts of the Body of Christ. Each part makes the other stronger and effective. A hand is no good without an arm, and a nose is no good without a face. (1 Cor. 12.) Your relationships are your key to your fulfillment and success.

I believe as your relationship with God grows through the truths of this book, your relationship with people will also grow. New friends, mentors, and partners will come to you, and you will find a whole new level of health and wholeness. Out of a good treasure in your heart you bring forth more and more good relationships and good things in life.

As we walk together through the message of this book, you will see yourself and others you know. It's not easy, but change is possible. Commit yourself to having a whole heart, and you are on your way to a higher level of life.

When God took the kingdom of Israel away from its first king, Saul, He said He was giving it to a better man. (1 Sam. 15:28.) Why was David a better man than Saul? Physically he wasn't as strong, tall, or good looking. His leadership skills had not been developed; he was only a boy who watched sheep and played the guitar. There was nothing in the physical or mental realm that showed David would be a better man or leader than Saul.

David was a better man because of his heart after God. (1 Sam. 13:14.) He desired to know God, serve God, obey God, and honor God. Even when he sinned, his desire was to get right and not lose his relationship with the Lord. He repented and cried out for a clean heart. (Ps. 51:10.) The heart condition of David made him a king, priest, and prophet. He was not perfect; in fact he failed many times. But his heart kept bringing him back to God, and he would repent and be cleansed.

You are probably like me, no extraordinary talents, skill, or accomplishments. But if we will have a heart after God, great things can happen in our lives. It's not our physical or intellectual abilities that will decide our future——it's our heart. Your future is in your heart. If you don't like what you know is in there, at this time be encouraged. As we go through the following chapters, you will learn how to change and renew your heart condition. This is not a quick change plan; it will take time and dedication, but it will produce positive and lasting results that affect every area of your life.

Questions

1. What problems in your life have led you to believe you have less than a healthy heart? (Matt. 12:35.)

2. What feelings do you have about yourself that have affected your discipline, drive, desire, and life in general?

3. Have you ever thought, *If it's God's will, it will happen?* How does that line up with Philippians 2:12?

4. Meditate on Luke 17:20-21. Consider your thoughts, intents, and feelings regarding your response to this powerful revelation.

2

Characteristics of the Human Heart

God wants every heart and every family to be whole, yet today over half of the young people in the world live in single-parent households during their early years. This often produces a heart within them that has been bruised, abandoned, rejected, or lied to.

Recently my son was snowboarding, and while doing jumps he fell on his shoulder and broke his collarbone. In such a situation he could have said, "I don't receive this," refused medical attention, and lived in denial and ignorance. The problem with that approach, though, is that his collarbone would not heal correctly.

However, if taken care of, it is a relatively simple break and only a matter of time for healing.

One of the signs of an orphaned heart is a refusal to look at personal problems and personal responsibility. When was the last time you looked at the attitudes and conditions in your heart? Whether you realize it or not, many of these were established by your childhood environment and carried into adulthood.

My wife recently met a man whose life exemplifies this well. During an airplane flight, he told my wife, Wendy, "I'm an atheist." They had a wonderful conversation about the Lord because the man was not *really* an atheist. His heart had been broken because he had been raised in a religion that had no healing for him. When he heard the truth about Jesus, he did believe and was open to God. Religion had left him empty and brokenhearted. Truth will set you free.

Your life experiences affect your heart. Time spent with a good family and church will produce positive results in your heart. Hurts, bitterness, and lies will produce problems in your heart.

As you learn God's Word and renew your mind with it, your heart recovers. Then as you make the necessary adjustments in your life, the problems in your heart will fade and you will begin to experience positive results. If you feel your life is on course with God, then all you need to do is make incremental changes and you will continue to grow, increase, improve, and prosper.

Think of it as driving to Los Angeles from Seattle. It's pretty much a straight shot south. Along the way you make incremental changes, like changing lanes now and then, but you are headed in the right direction. Don't stop. Don't give up. You will get there.

If your life has been a string of disasters and bad decisions, then stop the car, change your direction, and find the road that will take you to God's best for your life. These changes will take more than incremental changes or small adjustments. You may have to do a U-turn and get serious about making life changes.

It's Not Too Late

You may be thinking, *It's too late for me.* No, it's never too late. The man who introduced me to the Lord and helped me more than any person, other than my wife, was fifty years old when he began to seek God. He became a Christian at age fifty, was fifty-eight when I met him, and died at age sixty-four. In nine short years, Julius Young accomplished tremendous things for God. He was the key to my salvation.

It's never too late. You haven't gone too far. Julius was in prison at age fifty-five when he said, "Lord, if You save me, I will try to do something good with my life."

I thank God for Julius, my spiritual father. His fathering filled a hole in my heart that many people can identify with.

The lack of biblical fathering causes many people to struggle with inferiority, insecurity, and defensiveness. It causes us to say "I already know" when we don't even understand. It causes us to avoid change because if we have to change, we think that means there is something wrong with us. When you are insecure, you do not want to admit something is wrong.

At my natural father's funeral, I was reminded of a change that took place in my life when he divorced my mother. I was a teenager at the time of their divorce. He married the next-door neighbor. At that time I lost what little sense of right and wrong I had and was left with no sense of foundation or direction in my life.

Children whose fathers do not provide a biblical example often develop a broken, hurting, confused, and angry heart. Regardless of what your father has done, if you are an adult, it's too late to blame him or be angry. He did what he did. Maybe you are a dad still blaming your father for your problems. In reality, now you are responsible for your actions, and your children may grow up to blame you unless your heart is healed.

The feelings of inferiority and insecurity that develop in an orphaned heart hinder change and growth. You may stomp around and act like a tough guy when you feel insecure, inferior, and defensive. Others become quiet, withdrawn and hide because of their broken heart. This behavior develops calluses on your heart that hinder you from learning, growing, and changing.

The orphaned heart confines you to live in cycles of life that seem impossible to break out of. For example, you climb out of debt, but a year later you are right back in, deeper than before. You lose five pounds, only to gain ten more. You land a good job for a few months, until something happens and you are disappointed again. You constantly go through cycles of failure.

Whether it be relationships, finances, a physical need, or any other area, the heart is the control center. That is why, if your heart is orphaned, your life is broken; and if your heart is whole, your life is whole. You can overcome your inferiority when you *know* you are a creation of God. You can lay down your insecurities when you *know* the Lord will help you.

An inferior and insecure heart is consumed with what others think about it. However, we are all people facing the same challenges. So when you wonder what "they" think about you, the reality is that they are not thinking about you. They are thinking about what you think about them. We live in a society where we roll up our windows and drive down the freeway of life hoping no one gets in our lane, but we all deal with the same painful issues.

One such issue that many of us struggle with is our sense of value and self-worth, which comes from our parents, particularly our fathers. The feeling of being valuable is essential to mental health and is a corner-stone of self-discipline. A lack of self-discipline affects us in many ways. We live in a world that has very little self-discipline and we don't like delayed gratification. For instance, Americans seem to have more exercise equipment, diet pills, and fitness programs than anyone else on the planet does, yet obesity increases.

How can we have a closet full of bikes and rowing machines, a cupboard full of fat-burning pills and still gain weight? What is in our hearts determines what we do. A merry heart creates a healthy body, but a broken heart needs more Twinkies. A broken heart needs the "super size" fries.

For some, food is a drug; for others, money or alcohol is. The broken heart needs something to medicate the pain. I've been there as a patient and a pastor and have witnessed so many examples. To break these negative cycles, you must have your heart healed.

My love for my Grandfather Mac was one of the reasons I was able to make a change in my life that would lead toward a healed heart. My grandfather gave me a sense of value. I would spend every weekend with

Mac, talking with him, riding in his pickup truck, and eating candy. He bought me Boy Scout knives. He took me to Arizona, and we rode our motorcycles in the desert. He would always say, "You are my number one grandson," and he demonstrated that by hugging me and sitting with me in the big chair while we watched Lawrence Welk and *Gunsmoke.*

Unfortunately, I did not know God, and I had no biblical lifestyle. I ended up in drugs, alcohol, and crime, but deep inside I felt Grandpa Mac's words: "You are special. You are important. You are number one. You're my man. I love you."

When I became addicted to drugs, the *last* person whom I wanted to know about it was Grandpa Mac. The first time I was arrested, the first thing I said was "Please don't tell Grandpa." When I was placed on probation, I said, "Don't tell Grandpa." I knew he cared about me. I was ashamed and concerned that he would be disappointed in me.

I was about eighteen years old when my grandfather died. I was sad but also relieved. I didn't want him to know the mess I had made of my life. The love of someone you love in return affects your heart.

When Julius Young and I met at the Christian discipleship program, he said, "Big Red, you can change. You do not have to stay this way." I believed him because he believed in me, just as my Grandpa Mac had believed in me. Julius helped me receive a healed heart. In a matter of days, I was free from drugs, alcohol, and crime.

I never smoked another cigarette or joint or drank another beer. I never had another girlfriend until I found Wendy. Within a year of meeting Julius, I began Bible school; and within two years, I married my wife. Within four years, I became the pastor of a church. If you will pursue a whole heart, there is no limit to what God can do in your life.

Scott Peck writes in *The Road Less Traveled* about the heart and the lack of discipline that results from the problems of the heart.[1] Abandonment, rejection, or indifference from parents makes it difficult to become a strong, secure person.

Remember, the main problem for the orphaned heart is difficulty growing and changing. If a child is abandoned or orphaned, he or she becomes part of a government program and is passed from home to home. Children are vulnerable. They cannot buy their own food; someone must care for them, so they become members of foster families. They try to believe that someone is going to take care of them, but soon they are told, "You're too old for us," or "You're too big now." Then they go to the next place to be cared for. After two or three times of going through this, they develop an orphaned heart that wants love but is afraid of rejection. It's easy to become calloused.

The orphaned heart says, "I desperately want someone to love me, but I'm afraid I'm going to get hurt." It reaches out and pulls people close, then pushes them away before it gets hurt. The orphan's heart causes many to be very good at starting relationships but not able to make long-term commitments. The internal hurts prompt us to walk away before we get rejected or hurt again.

The mind-set of a person with an orphaned heart is the belief that good cannot last. When the subconscious fears take over, they begin to feel nervous. They begin to think, *I know something is going to happen.* When something does not happen, they manufacture the drama— because every one of us has the desire to defend our sanity. We must prove we are right, because if we are wrong, something must be wrong with us. They ruin the relationship and blame the other person.

The orphaned heart is spiritually weak and struggles with confidence in a heavenly Father because of difficulty with trust. In our present-day Christian movement, we can be more excited about Jesus than about the Father God because of the condition of our hearts. Jesus is a Friend; He is our Brother. We can relate to Jesus because of the personal, spiritual association we have. We resist the idea of a relationship with the Father because something in our hearts says fathers are not trustworthy.

Until we can relate to the heavenly Father, we cannot have all that God has provided for us. Jesus came to show us the Father. There are many manifestations of our lack of trust in our heavenly Father.

A person who does not tithe may be an example of an orphaned heart. He does not believe God will keep His Word. He does not believe he will receive "the windows of heaven" opened unto him. (Mal. 3:10.) He does not trust that 90 percent of his income with God's blessing on it is more than 100 percent without His blessing.

The orphaned heart says you have to get what you want and make sure no one takes it from you. It is an "I've got to stand on my own, pull myself up by my own boot-straps, not let any preacher or God or anyone else rip me off" mentality. Those thoughts produce a lack of trust in the heavenly Father and prevent your heart from healing.

The orphaned heart is often hungry for attention, approval, and validation. The individual with an orphaned heart will hunger for self-promotion. For example, he'll say, "You know what I did? I got the badge for the most sales last month," or she'll say, "I received this award because I was number one in the company."

We live in a society where medals, names, and titles make us feel important. Honorary degrees, though valid accomplishments for elderly people who are real states-men and women, for most are just a way to feel impor-tant. The orphaned heart searches for ways to show off accomplishments with a motivation for rewards. He fears failure and uses success as validation. He is devastated when failure comes and has a hard time getting back into the race.

The orphaned heart fears commitment, often saying yes out of a need to please, but then falls short on the follow-through. This person runs from long-term relationships or, when pressed in a relationship, often becomes emotionally unavailable.

In early years as the pastor of Christian Faith Center, I would become upset when people left the church. I could not understand it. I struggled. I stayed awake at night. I cried, "God, why did they leave? What did I do wrong? I must be a lousy pastor."

My friend Julius, my wife, Wendy, and others began to help me understand what was happening. My orphaned heart would become insecure if I felt someone did not like me or I was not good enough. I began to realize "This is not the way I want to live. I need to get my heart healed."

Often, people who come to church struggle with the same feelings of insecurity. You love them, teach them, pray for them, and care for them, but after a period of time they begin to think, *I've got to get on the road again.*

These people are going to get to know me. These relationships are going beyond the shallow level, and they are going to recognize me and want to come visit. I'm going to have to clean up my house. More importantly, I might have to clean up my heart. They become nervous because people become too close, so they begin to look for an escape.

It reminds me of when I was young and Mom would buy gas at the gas station, and they would give her S & H Green Stamps and a book to put them in. Mom would hand me the stamps, and I would lick them and put them in the book. The glue tasted good. When we filled the book, we cashed them in for a new toaster or some other item.

With this scenario in mind, say you've been attending church for a while, and people begin to know you. You start to feel like it's a little too intimate, so you start looking for things to criticize: "When I dropped the kids off this morning, the nursery worker had a bad attitude." "I walked into the sanctuary and sat down, and one of those ushers asked me to sit somewhere else." "The pastor's wife looked a little too cool."

You put a "stamp" in your book after each situation, and your book becomes half full. You create the rest in your mind: "I don't feel the same anointing that I felt when I first came." (Of course you don't. Your book of criticisms is half full of stamps.) "He's not teaching the way he used to teach." You place another stamp in your book. "I can't tell what it is, but there's something going on." So once your book is full, you mentally buy your way out of going to the church, and off you go to the next one.

But you won't be there long because you are a foster child. You go from house to house. Until the heart is made whole, you'll keep moving from place to place.

An orphaned heart looks for the quick fix and instant gratification: "I don't want to have to be faithful to the church. I'll just go to the special service and get a miracle." "Let's not get married. Let's just live together." "I don't want to have to be disciplined and save. I just want to borrow the money."

An orphaned heart medicates the pain of reality with drugs, alcohol, or anything that will dull the senses from the real world: "I don't want to live in my world. It's not

HEALING THE ORPHANED HEART

fun. I want to live in the major league baseball world. Give me a beer and a baseball game. I need a tranquilizer."

The orphaned heart uses anger and hostility to overpower the weaknesses it feels. It thinks, *If I just yell louder, I can win the argument.* It runs from one thing to another, looking for what only the heavenly Father can give—fulfillment and satisfaction.

The person with an orphaned heart questions those who love him and finds reasons to doubt them. "Pastor doesn't really care about me. He is just trying to get something for himself. The church does not care either. In fact, no one in the church cares. They're just trying to get something for themselves." If someone really cares for you, then you have no reason to run.

Now that we have seen the characteristics of an orphaned heart, let's discover the treasures of a whole heart. God wants you to have a whole heart that is open to the treasures of God's goodness.

Treasures in Your Heart

Some of us have a healthy heart. We have been reared in godly homes and have been taught to serve

God. We have walked with God to a degree, but we must continue with the lifestyle of a healthy heart in order to stay whole.

A whole, healthy, and strong heart will contain treasures that bring a successful life, a happy marriage, prosperous children, a business that prospers, and the ministry that God placed in your heart.

The healthy treasures in your heart will accomplish the destiny that God has established for you. At the end of your years on earth, you will be able to stand before the Lord and hear, "…Well done, good and faithful servant…" (Matt. 25:21).

Remember, Jesus said, "A good man out of the good treasure in his heart brings forth good things…" (Matt. 12:35).

The heart treasure starts with love. Many of us have the *concept* of love, but lack the *lifestyle* of love. A healthy heart loves God and people. There is no place for anger, hurt, or bitterness in a healthy heart.

You may say, "I agree with the concept of love," but when you walk into your office building, do you treat the receptionist with love? Do you offer a kind word or a genuine smile? When you go down the hallway, do you treat the maintenance guy with love, or do you respond, "Get your bucket out of my way"? We must stop the excuses. There is no excuse for anger or bitterness toward other human beings.

Recently I was tested on this issue at a fast-food drive-through. I started timing my wait in line: ten minutes...fifteen...twenty. I considered what I could say to the guy at the window, but before I got to the window, the Lord said to me, "What do you suppose the person behind the window is feeling right now?" I began to think about it: *Maybe these are young people who are stressed out because someone spilled the fries, turned off the grill, or didn't show up for work. And here comes another upset, angry customer.* So when I got to the window I said, "Praise the Lord" to the kid in the window. He just stared at me.

It's your decision. There is no reason to be mad, hateful, or upset. Whatever happens around you, God is inside you. You can handle a slow drive-through or the problems in your office. Yes, they are real; but if you want a whole heart, then you must build love into the treasure of your heart. Choose to love people as you love God: with all that is within you.

To get your love treasure right, believe and act upon Romans 5:5, which says, "...the love of God has been poured out in our hearts by the Holy Spirit who was given to us." The way to do this is to say, "I refuse to become angry, upset, or hateful. Love is within me, and I choose love." Then say a kind word instead of an angry one. Apply God's Word—the Bible—to your situation.

Healthy people with a whole heart are not anxious, nervous, or stressed out. Philippians 4:7 says, "And the peace of God, which surpasses all understanding, will guard your hearts and minds through Christ Jesus." Colossians 3:15 says, "And let the peace of God rule in your hearts, to which also you were called in one body; and be thankful." *The Amplified Bible* says, "And let the peace (soul harmony which comes) from Christ rule (act as umpire continually)...." In other words, let the peace of God call the shots.

Romans 5:1 says, "...we have peace with God through our Lord Jesus Christ." God knows all about you and everything in your world. If you have peace with God, then you can have peace with anyone. So make a decision to walk in that peace.

If you find yourself becoming upset, pounding your fist, and getting angry, back off. Let the peace of God guard, rule, reign, and be the umpire of your life.

People with a healthy heart practice peace and avoid relationships that are full of anxiety, stress, and manipulation. You may not "feel" peaceful, but realize it is your decision and choose to let your feelings follow the treasure of peace.

Run to Win

Discipline and self-control are qualities of a healthy heart. First Corinthians 9:24 says, "Do you not know that those who run in a race all run, but one receives the prize? Run in such a way that you may obtain it."

Paul essentially said, "If you are going to run the race of life, then *run to win*. If you are going to show up for the race, then plan to win it." If you are in church, then go for God. Look for God with all of your heart.

Paul goes on in 1 Corinthians 9:25: "And everyone who competes for the prize is temperate [disciplined] in all things. Now they do it to obtain a perishable crown, but we for an imperishable crown."

To play golf, you must train, prepare, control, and discipline your life. If you want to participate in any type of athletic endeavor, it takes discipline and self-control. The orphaned heart disciplines itself and learns self-control to participate in the "game of life" for a ring, a trophy, or a gold medal, but those with a healthy heart do it for an imperishable crown of glory in heaven.

> Therefore, I run thus: not with uncertainty. Thus I fight: not as one who beats the air.
>
> But I discipline my body and bring it into subjection, lest, when I have preached to others, I myself should become disqualified.
>
> 1 Corinthians 9:26,27

If the apostle Paul was concerned that if he didn't discipline his life he could lose the very thing he was taking to the world, then how much more serious should we be about a whole, healthy heart? This statement is not an attempt to make anyone feel afraid or condemned, but to encourage us to be realistic about maintaining a heart after God.

A disciple is a disciplined one.[2] We must stop making excuses and become disciplined. Refuse to compromise. We can overcome addictions to pornography, alcohol, and drugs by taking authority over them. We can overcome a negative tongue and control our mouth. We may think, *we can't help it,* and *we didn't mean it,* but we must make a heart change.

Because of a lack of discipline, some people find themselves in situations they never thought they would be in. You can't blame anyone for your own lack of discipline. Start with the small things and build discipline and self-control into the treasure of your heart.

Clothed With Humility

Humility is a quality of a healthy, whole heart. First Peter 5:5-6 says, "…Yes, all of you be submissive to one another, and be clothed with humility, for 'God resists the proud, but gives grace to the humble.' Therefore humble yourselves under the mighty hand of God, that He may exalt you in due time."

Scripture does not say God will humble you. It's religious tradition for preachers to say, "You'd better watch out or God is going to cut you down to size." That is not in the Bible. We must humble ourselves under the mighty hand of God, and He will exalt us.

"Pride goes before…a fall" (Prov. 16:18). To be humble, you must be honest with yourself. A little bit of reality can humble you.

Here is an illustration from my own life. Someone said to me recently, "Pastor, you must feel really proud. How do you keep your feet on the ground?"

I said, "Well, it's not very hard when I look at reality. We have six to seven thousand people in church and over a million in our area who do not come. We are not that big when you consider how many in our city still need Jesus."

I recently got a nice big slice of reality. One of the kids at Christian Faith Center came up to me and said, "Pastor, I'm inviting my baseball team to come to church with me."

One of the guys asked, "Where do you go to church?"

He said, "Christian Faith Center."

The other guy goes, "I've never heard of it."

People have not even heard of us.

Then the kid said to his baseball team, "You know, Casey Treat."

The kids said, "What's that, a candy bar?"

Humility can come quite naturally.

A healthy, whole heart has a sense of humility, value, and self-worth and does not need outward recognition. A servant does not need to be petted for helping. I've heard people say, "If I can't be an elder or have a position of authority, then I won't serve." The whole heart just wants to give and serve; the orphan's heart is looking for position.

David said, "...I would rather be a doorkeeper in the house of my God than dwell in the tents of wickedness" (Ps. 84:10).

Trust as a Child Trusts

We have to build the treasure of trust into our lives. We need to trust God and people. Proverbs 3:5 says, "Trust in the Lord with all your heart...."

I understand that when you trust people, you are disappointed sometimes. Jesus told us that if we want the blessing of the kingdom, we have to be like little children. Children are innocent. They have not been disappointed with others to the point that they become critical, paranoid, or suspicious.

Some people will take advantage of you when you are innocent, and you do not want to put yourself in a position to be hurt. I am not trying to imply that you should. However, trusting is better than living your life being suspicious, critical, careful, and cautious.

Do you trust yourself? Many people don't. Did you say you would read the Bible, but did not do it? Did you say you would lose five pounds, but didn't? You set the alarm but did not get up when it went off—that's why the snooze button is so big. If you don't do what you say you will do, you cannot trust yourself. And if you cannot trust yourself to keep your word, you cannot believe others will keep their word. When we become trustworthy, we find it easier to trust people. And we can grow in our trust of God.

One research study reveals that most Christians will call a professional for prayer, but they have no one else they can share with. They view the pastor as a doctor—the professional. They may call him for prayer, but they have no one else they trust. Their lives are closed and without relationships they really trust in times of crisis.

By building the treasure of trust in your heart, you bring forth the kind of relationships that are good, fulfilling, and rewarding. The best place to find such relationships is at church. "Those who are planted in the house of the Lord shall flourish…" (Psalm 92:13).

And remember, Christianity was not limited to the sanctuary in the early church. Acts 5:42 says, "And daily in the temple, and in every house, they did not cease teaching and preaching Jesus as the Christ." Their Christianity and fellowship were an everyday experience in every house. They built strong and trusting relationships.

Build Your Vision

God directs us to build vision into the treasure of our hearts. Proverbs 29:18 KJV says, "Where there is no vision, the people perish…." Where there is no vision, people go to jobs they don't like and die sooner than they should. Vision means "Here's what I can see for my future; here's what I believe I'm moving toward; here's what I expect to come to pass in my life."

It was while Jericho was shut up that the Lord gave Joshua his vision: "Jericho is yours."

> Now Jericho was securely shut up because of the children of Israel; none went out, and none came in.
>
> And the LORD said to Joshua: "See! I have given Jericho into your hand, its king, and the mighty men of valor."
>
> Joshua 6:1,2

The Israelites knew of their Promised Land, but they had to cross the river Jordan to possess it. They knew the land flowed with milk and honey, but the first step into that new property was God's word "I have given you Jericho." You have to see your Jericho before you can possess it.

The Lord once spoke to me and said, "Many people want a vision for success in life, an abundant life, a prosperous life, but they can't see their first victory." We want a vision of a happy family, but we cannot even visualize a successful family relationship. We do not have a vision of praying with our spouse and children with the expectation of a positive result. See the first step. You must see your Jericho and possess it before you can take your Promised Land. You must see the beginning steps and then develop a vision for long-term success.

Some men can't visualize taking their wife out on a date and experiencing nice, intimate conversation. If you cannot imagine one good evening with your wife, there is no way you are going to have a vision for a successful marriage. You have to build the treasure of vision into your heart.

Start with vision. Get the picture of the result you want. Obtain a vision for happy fellowship and communion with your spouse. See your family sitting down to a nice time of prayer and intimacy; then your bigger vision will happen. Say, "I'm going to conquer. I am going to overcome. I'm going to prosper." Build up that treasure in your heart.

The next step to building the treasures of your heart is to build a love, acceptance, and excitement for responsibility. The reality is that we live in a world that shirks responsibility. We sign papers so we will not be liable. At the doctor's office, we sign documents declaring, "Whatever might happen, the doctor is not responsible." Recently I stayed at a hotel, and before I could use the gym I had to sign a contract that said the hotel would not be responsible for any injuries to me. In the legal world, our fear of liability causes us to avoid responsibility.

Everyone seems to be hiding from responsibility. Some people have attended our church and when we asked them to help in a particular area, they said, "I'd love to help, but I can't take on any more responsibility."

Many times we avoid responsibility because of fear and wrong treasures of the heart. It is time to build new treasures. Become excited about the privilege and opportunity of responsibility. It is a great thing to be responsible for your family, your children, and others in your church.

Imagine if God had turned to the Lord Jesus Christ eons ago and said, "Someone's got to go save those people because they are lost in their sin," and Jesus said, "I can see some added responsibility coming My way, and I just want You to know right now, I am not responsible for the sins of Adam." Jesus didn't say that. His heart embraced responsibility for our salvation.

Whose lives are you embracing responsibility for? What are you doing that they might be saved? Whom are you praying for, serving, and helping, that their lives can be affected? When the treasure in your heart is right, you will search for areas you can take responsibility in.

The Joy of the Lord

Joy is part of the treasure in the heart of every Christian. Christianity has not always had a reputation for being a lot of fun. Our music, buildings, atmosphere, and preachers have not always been "up." In the past, it was unusual to go to a church that was upbeat. Religion in general is usually sad and depressed.

Nevertheless, the joy of the Lord is a privilege and an exciting part of Christianity. Furthermore, joy is vital to the fulfillment of your destiny. There is not enough energy in depression to propel you into your destiny; you need the strong force of joy.

Jesus said, "These things I have spoken to you, that My joy may remain in you, and that your joy may be full" (John 15:11). He did not mean we would be happy all the time. Sometimes we have difficult decisions to make, responsibilities to assume, and issues to solve. However, in the midst of life's challenges, part of the treasure of our hearts is a sense of joy.

Joy is evident when you have a healed heart. You know your destiny. You experience a solid foundation on the Word of God. Can you imagine living in the world without a sense of where you are going, unable to make decisions, not knowing right from wrong?

Joy doesn't come from the outside in. It must flow from the inside out. Some people cycle through jobs and relationships because they are searching for something or someone that makes them feel good. As we walk with the Lord, His joy will rise up in our lives. Nehemiah 8:10 says, "The joy of the Lord is your strength." Joy does not follow emotions; emotions follow joy. When you make a decision that "the joy of the Lord is your strength," the Holy Spirit will begin to make this true in your life.

Choose joy. When you have family issues to talk about, say, "Thank God we are Christians, and we are together. We have some issues to talk about, but let's not forget that the joy of the Lord is our strength. We are not going to get mad, upset, or mean. We are going to stay in the joy of the Lord."

Now, with a better understanding of both an orphaned heart and the treasures God has made available to us, let's enter the process of developing a healthy and whole heart.

Questions

1. How have inferiority and low self-esteem affected your life? (Eph. 2:10.)

2. Did your father/parents give you a sense of value, dignity, and destiny? (Eph. 6:4.)

3. Check yourself according to the characteristics of an orphaned heart. Realize that through the Word of God and the Holy Spirit, you can overcome any limitations in your life.

3

⮾

Becoming Aware of Ourselves

As I mentioned in Chapter two, one of the symptoms of an orphaned heart is a refusal to look at the matters of the heart. The first step toward a whole heart is to become aware of your heart condition.

First Corinthians 11:28 says, "But let a man examine himself, and so let him eat of the bread and drink of the cup." Every time you take communion, which should be a part of your lifestyle, examine yourself. Paul goes so far as to say in verses 29-30:

> For he who eats and drinks in an unworthy manner eats and drinks judgment to himself, not discerning the Lord's body.

For this reason many are weak and sick among you, and many sleep.

If we ignore our spiritual heart condition, we become weak and sick, and we die prematurely. If we examine our lives, become aware of what is going on, and become honest with the Lord, then we can be healed and strengthened and enjoy long lives.

Unfortunately, many fail to examine their hearts and, therefore, miss out on these blessings. The wife of a friend of ours recently died of cancer. The husband is a leader in the body of Christ and has ministered in our church and around the world. The doctor told us, "This could have been avoided. It was due to stress and anxiety. It was about physical and emotional fitness. This kind of cancer does not have to take lives. Usually we can deal with it and overcome it."

We need to become aware of our heart condition. Many people live with confusion, discord, and anxiety in their hearts. How can we agree with our spouse, pastor, or the Lord when we cannot even agree with ourselves?

Wholeness carries a connotation of unity and agreement. A whole heart is one without strife, confusion, and disagreement.

> Let not mercy and truth forsake thee: bind them about thy neck; write them upon the table of thine heart:
>
> So shalt thou find favour and good understanding in the sight of God and man.
>
> Trust in the Lord with all thine heart; and lean not unto thine own understanding.
>
> In all thy ways acknowledge him, and he shall direct thy paths.
>
> Be not wise in thine own eyes: fear the Lord, and depart from evil.
>
> It shall be health to thy navel, and marrow to thy bones.
>
> Honour the Lord with thy substance, and with the firstfruits of all thine increase:
>
> So shall thy barns be filled with plenty, and thy presses shall burst out with new wine.
>
> Proverbs 3:3-10 KJV

We must develop unity, harmony, and peace in the inner man. Agreement is the place of power. Matthew 18:18-19 KJV says, "Verily I say unto you, Whatsoever ye shall bind on earth shall be bound in heaven: and whatsoever ye shall loose on earth shall be loosed in heaven.

Again I say unto you, That if two of you shall agree on earth as touching any thing that they shall ask, it shall be done for them of my Father which is in heaven." There must be agreement within your own heart.

In the natural, you can have problems with your ankles, knees, or elbows; your jaw can lock up; your ears can ring. But your heart keeps ticking, so you learn to deal with it or overcome it, and you move forward. But if your heart stops pumping, you're dead.

You may not know what is going on in your natural heart until one day the chest pains hit, and you have a heart attack, fall on the floor, and grab your chest. You are rushed to the hospital; the doctor takes a knife and slices you right down the middle, reaches into your chest cavity, and massages life back into your heart. Your heart is the center of the flow of life in your body.

The Bible says, "The life of every creature is its blood…" (Lev. 17:14 NIV). That is why blood was always part of the Old Testament sacrifices and why Jesus had to give His blood for our salvation. Your heart pumps blood to every part of your body.

Unawareness of the physical condition of the heart causes many people to die young. Doctors encourage us to learn about good diet and health habits so we will not die prematurely from heart problems.

The same thing is true for our spiritual hearts. Maybe you have allowed spiritual cholesterol into your heart. You may not realize that in the early years of life you were hurt when Dad left or when Mom and Dad divorced. You put some of that hurt into your heart, and it caused injury.

Maybe you did not realize that when you were in school and were told we are descendants of chimpanzees, accidents of nature, or mutations of evolution, those lies stole some of your value and self-esteem.

Maybe you did not recognize that as a young woman, when that young man made out with you and you rejected him and the next day he rejected you, it damaged your heart.

Maybe when you were seeking an abortion, you were not told it would change your life forever. The residue and pain of abortion remains in your heart, and now your heart is incomplete.

We do not realize all the spiritual cholesterol that builds up in our hearts from the hurts, failures, pains, problems, and negative words. We think that throughout our lives we were really unaffected, as one thinks his natural diet does not affect him that much—until the heart attack comes.

When my dad died, his family was unaware that he had experienced any prior problems. He never said anything. One day we went out to the barn and found him sitting on the floor with his back against the door of the stall. He had left his body. Upon examination, his family learned he'd had a heart attack. There had been no warning. He'd been a young, thin, healthy, and handsome man.

If you are unaware of your spiritual heart condition, your heart will bring forth things that you did not even know were there.

What happens when a couple who have been together for ten or more years suddenly divorce? One woman shared with me after a service, "After years of marriage, my husband said to me, 'I'm leaving you.'"

She had not thought it would ever happen to her. She suffered a spiritual heart attack.

I worked with a family that had been in ministry for twenty years. They had a good church and were godly people. In this case, the wife left the kids and her husband.

With no warning, cholesterol builds up day after day, and the spiritual heart attack follows—if you do not examine your heart. People who have heart disease say, "I never thought it would happen to me." If you are unaware and do not know what is going on in your heart, then when that heart attack hits, what happens as a result will come as a complete surprise.

Awareness keeps our hearts flowing. We must make sure our spiritual heart is full of the truth of God's Word, lest a spiritual heart attack take us out of His blessings (due to a lack of knowledge of His Word).

In 1 Thessalonians 5:23 Paul says, "Now may the God of peace Himself sanctify you completely; and may your whole spirit, soul, and body be preserved blameless at the coming of our Lord Jesus Christ." God does not want you to be born again and just hang on until the Rapture. He wants your spirit, soul, and body to be healed and whole. God wants you to live a successful life that brings honor and glory to Him.

In Matthew 15 the scribes and Pharisees question Jesus because the disciples have failed to wash their hands before eating. Jesus is not impressed with their question, so He confronts them with their behavior and lifestyle. In verse 8 Jesus says, "These people draw near to Me with their mouth, and honor Me with their lips, but their heart is far from Me."

It is one thing to say the religious things you have heard others say, but it's another thing to really have a relationship with God inside your heart. Jesus confronted these hypocrites because they talked religious talk, but their hearts were not right with Him.

Jesus said:

> "But those things which proceed out of the mouth come from the heart, and they defile a man.
>
> "For out of the heart proceed evil thoughts, murders, adulteries, fornications, thefts, false witness, blasphemies.
>
> "These are the things which defile a man, but to eat with unwashed hands does not defile a man."
>
> Matthew 15:18-20

God told us our problems in life come out of our hearts. Adultery does not happen by accident. It starts in the heart—not on purpose and not because someone is evil, but somewhere in development it contaminates the heart.

When the wrong things contaminate your heart, you do things that will embarrass you later in life. I can remember doing things that I was embarrassed about and ashamed of later. I would say, "Why did I do that?" I did it because it was in my heart.

The Christian parent who abuses his child hates himself for it, but the action comes out of his heart. The Christian who ends up in sin is ashamed, but it comes from what's in the heart. What is in your heart? It will appear in your behavior.

Some people have said, "I don't want to go to a church that makes me examine my heart. I want a church that makes me feel good." Do not allow church to serve as only a way to make you feel better. You want to *be* better. Sitting in a pew will not make you closer to God. Religious functions do not make you strong. The real issues of the heart determine who you are.

If you have cancer in your body, surgery will hurt a bit, but you will be glad to have the cancer removed. A trip to the dentist is not fun when he takes out his drill to remove the decay, but you are glad when you smile and those cavities are gone. Likewise, it is not fun to examine your heart, but the positive results will be worth it all.

Some Christian girls flirt and flaunt themselves because of insecurity in their hearts. The flesh says flaunting and flirting will get you what you want and take you where you want to go. Somehow that crept into their hearts.

Maybe there is loneliness and separation in your heart. If you examine your heart issues, you will discover what God can do with your life. You can find out what it is like to walk with God.

In the financial arena we see many who believe in prosperity and listen to prosperity teaching but are unable to pay their bills. They confess, "God gives me the power to get wealth. God meets all of my needs according to His riches in glory by Christ Jesus," but continue to drive that rattletrap piece of junk and take their wife home to a house that embarrasses her. Poverty is still in their heart.

When your heart is whole, prosperity will flow. When your heart is healed, relationships will become easy. Beauty flows out of a whole heart. You will not have to paint it on and flaunt it. It will be a natural part of your life when your heart is whole. When your soul prospers, you will prosper in all things. (3 John 2.)

Face Reality

No one has arrived. We do not have it all together. The apostle Paul said:

> ...one thing I do, forgetting those things which are behind and reaching forward to those things which are ahead,
>
> I press toward the goal for the prize of the upward call of God in Christ Jesus.
>
> Philippians 3:13,14

We are all in the same process of learning about ourselves, getting our hearts healed, becoming more like Jesus, and trying to live life according to God's will and His Word. We all need to find out what negative things are in our heart; otherwise, those things will defeat us. We must be honest with ourselves in order to be free.

As you become aware of the issues in your heart and recognize the ungodly attitudes in it, ask God for healing and a new spirit of the heart. Repent for allowing your past to rule your heart. You are a new creature. Confess the change. Believe you receive new, godly treasures in your heart—love, peace, joy, and so forth. Practice your new heart treasures in thought, word, and deed.

Make an honest confession right now: "Lord, I'm not going to hide. I'm not going to lie. I'm not going to deny. I'm not going to avoid. I open the door of my heart and ask You to come in and make it whole. I want a new heart, a healed heart, and a whole heart, in the name of Jesus. I am going to guard and keep my heart, for out of it flow the issues of life. Thank You, Father, for removing every negative, unbiblical thought from my heart, in Jesus' name."

Questions

1. Are there hurts, failures, pains, problems, and negative words you still hold in your heart? Identify them and ask for forgiveness of yourself and others. (1 Thess. 5:23.)

2. Do you hear things come out of your mouth that don't agree with God's picture of who you are and what your life should reflect of Him? (Eph. 5:1.)

3. Make a list of the things that still bother you from your past. Give your past to the Lord. Crumple up that list and throw it away. It no longer belongs to you. (Phil. 3:13,14.)

4

Renewing the Spirit of the Mind

Once you become aware of your heart condition, you must renew your mind to what God's Word, the Bible, says about your life. Most of our struggles we have with the mind are not conscious problems. They are part of the spirit of our mind, or the subconscious. Without our even realizing it, they rise out of our hearts.

In Ephesians 4:22-24 Paul says:

> …that you put off, concerning your former conduct, the old man which grows corrupt according to the deceitful lusts,
>
> and be renewed in the spirit of your mind,

and that you put on the new man which was created according to God, in true righteousness and holiness.

Notice the phrase "the spirit of your mind." This is a reference to the subconscious mind, below the conscious level.

The average Christian doesn't even know what the spirit of the mind is, so how can we renew the spirit of our mind? Yet Paul said that if you are not renewed in the spirit of your mind, if you do not "put on the new man," you never really live the new life.

Many people accept less than God's best. They are on their way to heaven, but they do not have God's will "on earth as it is in heaven." They try to avoid their former selves, stop old problems, and overcome old behaviors, but they never accept their new nature. They struggle with the carnality and negativity of their world because they do not understand the renewal of the spirit of the mind.

This process applies to the deep, subconscious parts of your heart. Please be aware that sensitive subjects that come up during this process must not be overanalyzed. Do not try to create problems or imagine things that are not there. Take an *honest* look at issues that come to your mind, make a decision about how you want to deal with them, and move forward with the Lord's guidance.

You have to get to the deep, "spirit of the mind" issues to have a whole heart and a whole life. These issues affect every area of your life, from your relationships to your physical health. The Bible says that a merry heart is the medicine of your flesh. (Prov. 17:22.)

When you renew your mind, you *know* what God said and you choose to think His way and do His Word. A person with a renewed spirit of the mind knows and does what God says. We must go beyond doing what we should do and start wanting to do what is right because the right answer is in our hearts.

Many try to renew their mind by forcing themselves to do what is right, but not because their heart wants to. If we compared the heart to autopilot on an airplane, it's as if these people manually override the autopilot. However, when they relax or lose focus, when they return to their real thinking, the old autopilot takes over. They are back on the old course of life and may not even realize it.

When the spirit of your mind is not renewed, your orphaned heart causes you to sabotage your life. You make choices that hurt you instead of staying in God's blessing.

Roots of the Heart

The "roots" of your heart produce positive and negative results. Hebrews 12:15 says, "...looking diligently [becoming aware, plugging in, learning] lest anyone fall short of the grace of God [or live below God's will, His grace, His blessing]; lest any root of bitterness springing up cause trouble, and by this many become defiled."

Bitterness means "b. a bitter root... producing a bitter fruit."[1]

Springing comes from the Greek word *phuo* meaning "to 'puff' or blow" or "to swell up."[2]

Defile means "...to taint" or "contaminate."[3] A bitter root from negative circumstances in life swells up and contaminates our hearts.

How does a marriage fail after a couple has been together for a number of years? A root springs up. How do people end up in debt and poverty after knowing the promise of God's prosperity? A root springs up. How do we accept a depressed, discouraged lifestyle when we are full of the Spirit of God, the joy of the Lord belongs to us, and the peace of the Lord is ours? A root defiles our hearts. It keeps us from God's best.

Roots are below the surface. We see the tree trunk, leaves, and branches on the conscious, surface level. When you renew the spirit of your mind to God's best for your life, you are willing to dig up the negative roots and move toward a healed, whole heart.

The roots of your life, the issues in your heart, predict your future. It will not work to cover up, ignore, or deny them. Down the road, you will have a big garbage dump of issues that have never been dealt with.

What happens when truckload after truckload, acre after acre of garbage has been dumped in one area? Let's say one day the city says, "This thing is full," and covers it over with topsoil. After they cover the garbage, they plant some beautiful grass and everybody says, "We've got a new park." It looks so nice on the surface. After a few short years, neighbors begin to experience headaches and physical problems. It is determined that methane gas is rising through the grass, so an elaborate system of piping is built to deal with the problem. The gases are gathered and burned off so the gas will not escape into the atmosphere.

You can cover the garbage of your past, but it will not heal your heart. When you come to church you may look nice, but gases are rising from the surface below. They are personality disorders. You love the Lord, you are on your way to heaven, but you still cannot get your relationships right. You trust God, you believe in God, you work hard, but you still struggle financially.

Maybe you believe the Bible and you quote Scripture, but you cannot serve others or get close to them. You feel lonely, isolated, and separated. You call yourself a Christian, but you do not have time for your children, you talk disrespectfully about your husband, and you gossip to your neighbors. You have believed in the Lord for years but have never introduced one person to Jesus. You barely find time to pray.

We can look good on the outside, but the hurts, pains, and problems of our past are bringing up gases. There is a tendency to blame others and point the finger.

We want to say, "It's that spouse who left me," "It's that guy who raped me," "It's that parent who rejected me." Certainly they had a part to play, but *you* have to decide right now if you want a whole, healthy, healed heart.

God gives you opportunities to be healed, to be renewed in the spirit of your mind, and to deal with those roots. Become aware, and decide not to hide what you can't hide anyway. Natural roots can be very powerful; they can grow right up through the cement and tear a roadway to pieces. They can spring up no matter how much concrete you put on top of them. Spiritual roots have a way of coming up when you least expect them. Be determined not to ignore or deny them or stay away from church to hide them.

Perhaps bad roots are affecting your marriage. Many marriage disagreements are not because of conscious decisions. They are the result of subconscious beliefs and attitudes. We display an attitude and react to something our spouse said and cannot rationally explain our reaction. Our habits and attitudes are linked to a root system in our lives. In the natural, sometimes you can pull up one root and realize it has gone way over to the other side of the yard. It is not so easy to get rid of. Likewise, in the spirit realm, we must begin to look below the surface of our lives.

Biblical Self-Esteem

We must see ourselves through God's eyes by renewing our minds with the Word of God.

> And do not be conformed to this world, but be transformed by the renewing of your mind, that you may prove what is that good and acceptable and perfect will of God.
>
> For I say, through the grace given to me, to everyone who is among you, not to think of himself more highly than he ought to think, but to think soberly, as God has dealt to each one a measure of faith.
>
> For as we have many members in one body, but all the members do not have the same function,
>
> so we, being many, are one body in Christ, and individually members of one another.
>
> Having then gifts differing according to the grace that is given to us, let us use them....
>
> Romans 12:2-6

Paul essentially said, "The first thing you've got to change is how you think about yourself. Realize you are part of the body of Christ. You have been given the measure of faith and gifts that are valuable and important.

We are to view ourselves from God's perspective and not think more highly of ourselves than we ought to think. At the same time, we are not to think more lowly of ourselves than we ought to think. We are to think soberly.

I think it would be safe to say that many men allow their pride and ego to decide how they view themselves. Most wouldn't go to another man and discuss personal issues. The inability to share with a Christian brother often results from a self-image built on fear, anxieties, and insecurities.

Insecurity and fear can cause you to come across as stoic and closed. A self-image based on weakness is not internally healthy. Inner turmoil can be avoided if you renew your mind to the ways of God.

God wants you to realize that you possess unique gifts and talents, but you are also one member of the body of Christ. You cannot and don't have to do anything alone. My hand has great talents, but without an arm it is useless. Every member of the body is to help the other members. To grow and change, it takes intimate relationships.

Some of us do not know who we are. We think we are accidents of nature, or freaks of evolution. You should know that there is a purpose for your life. You are made in the likeness and image of God. You are His son or daughter. You can know who you are from a biblical perspective.

It's hard to have peace and joy if you are frustrated with what you do every day of your life. Many people have asked, "How do I know if I'm in God's will? How do I know if my work is God's will for my life?" If you examine your work and find satisfaction in a job well done, then you are on the right track. If you are unable to rejoice or if you feel uncommitted, then it may be time to make a change. If you are going to spend forty, fifty, or sixty hours a week doing something, you should be able to look back at your work and say, "I can rejoice in it."

When considering your destiny and your career, the question you need to answer is *What can I do and rejoice in, find satisfaction in, and be excited about?*

Maybe you care for ten babies in your daycare. You nurture them in a protected, safe environment. Every day you can rejoice because there are ten families who do not have to send their children to the world for daycare. They can work without fear of what may happen to their children. You plant seeds of Scripture into these children. Who would think a daycare is a big thing? You can rejoice in yourself alone, not comparing yourself to anyone else, and say, "Thank You, Father, I am right where You want me to be."

Maybe you are writing computer programs and dealing with computer analyses and issues, and you are a positive influence in your workplace. Your work is one of integrity, and you are making a positive contribution to your workplace. You are investing your salary into your family and your church. At the end of the week you say, "Thank You, Lord. I get to do what I enjoy, and I am paid to do it. Life is good."

If your mother wanted you to be a pastor and you are a pastor because of her, you can feel good about helping people and teaching the Word. However, if at the end of the week you are stressed out, sad, and miserable, then you have to be honest with yourself. You are either not doing it right, or you are not doing the right thing. You shouldn't be doing something because someone else thinks it is noble or worthy; do what God has shown you to do, and you'll be able to rejoice in it.

Who you are and what you do affect your self-esteem. When you can rejoice in yourself, you will begin to have security, peace, joy, and a relaxed life. You can know purpose for your life.

Maybe you've become a Christian or you've learned more about God's plan for your life, so you've aimed toward a new destination, a new sense of life, a new level. You've decided to go to a higher level economically and relationally. Every step takes you to the next level. Do not lose that focus. As long as you are conscious and taking charge of your life, you can eliminate behaviors of the old nature.

What Do You Want?

Will you be healed, or will you stay sick? Jesus asked people, "What do you want?" If they didn't make a choice, there was nothing He could do for them. The

Lord had to ask them to activate their will before He could activate a miracle.

You must activate your will if you want a whole heart. Over half the process is deciding "I'm not going to live my life scared, bitter, resentful, with broken relationships, and unwilling to forgive. I'm not going to live my life with an unhealthy heart."

You have a right to a whole heart. Choose to renew your mind to the Word of God. In the next chapter, we will explore the power of your will.

Questions

1. What behaviors or attitudes have you tried to change but they keep hanging around in your life? (Eph. 4:22.)

2. Do you have issues you have tried to ignore, cover, hide, or lie about?

3. Are there things you believe God wants you to do but you cannot break through and do?

4. Are there new thoughts or behaviors you have been able to start, only to slip back into your old way of thinking and acting?

5. What thoughts or emotions are in the back of your mind that may be causing this response?

5

⤜⤛⤛

The Power of Your Will

As you work toward a healthy and whole heart, you develop the ability to make good choices and exercise willpower. You have a powerful will, and how you use it will affect your eternity and, to a great degree, your life on earth.

Genesis 1:26 says that you were made in the image and likeness of God. God is a Spirit, and we are spirit beings. I believe part of what makes us like God is our will—our ability to choose.

In Luke 10:40-42, Jesus says that Mary chose the good part.

> And Jesus answered and said unto her, Martha, Martha, thou art careful and troubled about many things:

But one thing is needful: and Mary hath chosen that good part, which shall not be taken away from her.

Luke 10:41,42

We will discuss this at length a little later in the chapter, but what I want you to notice right now is that Jesus said she chose.

As we established in Chapter one, your heart is your inner man, which includes your thoughts, feelings, emotions, and will—or ability to choose. All of these components make up your heart.

The will is like a muscle. It can be developed and strengthened. It can be trained to do whatever you want it to do. It is a tremendous gift, and it makes you God-like in the sense that you control your eternal destiny with it.

You decide with your will whether you will live with God forever or reject Him. You determine whether you will be in His Presence or be separated from Him. No one can make that decision for you. Satan cannot, God will not, and no other human being can.

The power of the human will must be exercised every day. You may not feel like making the right choice, but you can daily choose the things that keep your heart healthy. You can daily choose to be a spiritual, positive, healthy, godly person. Good choices come in daily decisions.

Things can happen beyond our choice, but even then we choose how to deal with those issues, and the outcome is still determined through those choices. For example, say a man asks a woman out on a date and her immediate response is "Yes, I'm looking for a man and want a relationship." A strong, godly woman would think first and choose to find out about his spiritual foundation, whether he is saved and serving God. She would ask about the church he attends; and if he is not in God's kingdom, in a church, and serving the Lord, it makes no sense to her to go out with him. If she determines he is a Christian, then she knows to find out "Are you interested in a future, a long-term relationship, or do you just want sex? What are your intentions in asking me out? I'm a strong, godly woman, looking for destiny, relationship, and a future." She would take the time to make a wise choice.

Consider every positive choice a health bar that strengthens your heart. The strong will is not controlled by what is popular or easy. The whole, healthy heart sets its course according to God's will instead of the majority.

You can view every negative choice as a Twinkie that weakens your will. Those people controlled by peer pressure have a weak will and an unhealthy heart. Habits of compromise keep many from God's best.

Often it seems so much easier to choose what opposes the Word of God. It's like lunch in the break room at an office: Sometimes the only thing around is junk food from a machine. Inside the machine is a nice, fat cupcake. It looks so good and has such clever wrapping. It is soft and moist and has creamy white filling. How can it be wrong when it looks so right? You can almost taste it.

It is so easy to obtain junk food. It is on every corner, in every store, everywhere you go. A health bar is not only harder to find, but it may also be much harder to open. I used to eat health bars when I raced bicycles. I almost fell off my bike trying to open one. Once I got it open, it was difficult to eat. Try to eat one of those things when you are out of breath!

To obtain something healthy, you have to search for it; you have to work for it. You have to use your willpower to pass on the cupcake and go for the health bar. The same is true for spiritual food for the heart.

When eating out, if you were a healthy, disciplined, physically fit person, what would you choose from the restaurant menu? You might want to have a 12-ounce T-bone with a side of french fries and a double-decker chocolate shake, but if you're a healthy, physically fit, disciplined person on your way to living 120 years, you'll have vegetables, a salad, and a glass of water.

Likewise, you have to develop choices that produce a healthy heart. You have to daily choose to be a positive, godly person. For a couple of years after I became a Christian, I did not feel like making right choices. I kept saying to myself, "If I were a good Christian, what would I choose?" I did that for so long that I accidentally began to make good choices! My mentor and spiritual dad, Julius, used to say, "You know, Casey, you keep faking long enough, you are going to trick yourself." I tricked myself right into holiness. When you don't feel like making the right choice, do it anyway.

Life Is Full of Choices

It takes daily discipline to make positive choices. It is your choice to live with blessing or die with cursing. The Lord cannot force it on you. You choose to be blessed or cursed, happy or sad, rich or poor.

Deuteronomy 30:19 says, "I call heaven and earth as witnesses today against you, that I have set before you life and death, blessing and cursing; therefore choose life, that both you and your descendants may live."

Every aspect of life is a choice. It is up to your will. We often make choices that we forget about, and years down the road those choices become habits that we are no longer aware of choosing. We start saying things like "I can't help it. It's just the way I am. It's in my DNA." Years down the road, what once was a choice is so automatic, so rooted into our lives, that we see it as something that just happened.

Take smoking for example. Maybe you stole your dad's Chesterfields with no filter, snuck out behind the house, and lit up. You put a fire on one end, a fool on the other, and you started sucking. Why did you? You chose to. No one held a gun to your head or forced you to smoke that cigarette. You chose to. Perhaps your dad smoked or your mom smoked. Cool people you knew and admired smoked, and you wanted to be like them.

Your first puff left you dizzy and green. You thought, *Why did I do that?* Your first try made you sick, but you wanted to be cool. You sucked it up repeatedly until it no longer made you sick. You learned how to hold the cigarette and how to put up with your mouth tasting like an ashtray. You learned how to buy them, get money to purchase them, and you became a smoker. You made that choice repeatedly until it became an addiction.

Then you were born again and filled with the Holy Spirit. You almost smoked Him out. You decided, "I've got to stop this. I am going to quit smoking. This is crazy. I want to live a long life, and I am tired of smelling like an ashtray. I've got to stop."

You want to stop, but now it's not easy because smoking has become a habit. There are some physical reasons for your addiction, but the physical reasons are minimal compared to the heart reasons. You made that choice so often that it's rooted down in your heart. Just as you can develop a root of bitterness, you can also develop a root of an addiction, a habit, and a behavior, and it is very hard to stop.

Choose the "Good Part"

Throughout history there are examples of people who have tried to dominate the wills of other people. It just cannot be done. There are a few documented occasions when people have submitted and surrendered. Most often, though, a human being will never surrender his will. The will is an extremely powerful force.

Perhaps the greatest example occurred during World War II, when the Nazis herded the Jewish people into camps, where they were tortured and forced to submit to medical and psychological experiments. The Nazis did everything they could to break the will of the Jewish people. In most cases, it made the Jews even stronger. It gave them more resolve. They emerged from World War II to fight for their own land and establish their own nation. The human will is powerful.

Luke 10:38-42 says:

Now it happened as they went that He entered a certain village; and a certain woman named Martha welcomed Him into her house.

And she had a sister called Mary, who also sat at Jesus' feet and heard His word.

But Martha was distracted with much serving, and she approached Him and said, "Lord, do You not care that my sister has left me to serve alone? Therefore tell her to help me."

And Jesus answered and said to her, "Martha, Martha, you are worried and troubled about many things.

"But one thing is needed, and Mary has chosen that good part, which will not be taken away from her."

It appeared as if Martha was doing well. She was a helper and a servant, always the one to clean the table, wash the dishes, and take care of everyone. However, she was not happy doing it. She performed her duties with a negative attitude; and the more she did, the angrier she became, until roots of resentment began to grow on the inside of her heart.

A heart can grow hard with thoughts like *I've been picking up after you for twenty-five years,* or *I've been putting up with your sloppiness for twelve years.* You may be great at taking care of the children and looking after the household, but if you do it with a negative attitude, then your heart will grow hard.

Finally, Martha couldn't take it anymore, and she went to Jesus. She essentially said to Jesus, "Do something about my lazy sister. I'm the only one around here who cares."

Jesus said, "Martha, this isn't your only problem. Mary is not the issue. You are distracted, troubled, and worried about many things."

It may not be your spouse, the job, the housework, or the children; it could be many things that are troubling you. Perhaps you have allowed your heart to become mean, bitter, angry, or fearful.

Jesus said, "...Mary has chosen that good part, which will not be taken away from her." Martha was the way she was *by choice*. You are the way you are *by choice*. Choose the good part.

All Martha had to do was say, "You mean I'm running around here all uptight, worried, and stressed out because of my own choices?"

Jesus would have said, "Yes, Martha, you need to start choosing a different lifestyle."

"Well, okay, I'm just going to sit down and listen to the Word of God."

If your heart is willing to change, you will see the truth of what is in your heart and use your will to choose what is good. Develop that muscle to make good choices to overcome the poor choices of the past. Retrain and exercise your willpower to choose the good part.

Do not let anyone take away the good. It is easy to find cheap relationships and shallow people. It is easy to meet people who don't care about anything that lasts. If you want a real, deep relationship, you have to search for it with patience.

Why does the relationship that you fantasized you would have with your spouse seem so much better than the one you have? It's because the cheap, shallow images of the world look attractive. Everything appears to be nice and soft and to feel good. In reality, those relationships are counterfeits of the relationship God has to offer.

You have tremendous willpower to choose either God's best or the world's counterfeit. Use it. Someone once said, "You may think you don't have very good willpower, but you do. You fought hard to stay the way you are. You have strong willpower. The question is, what are you using your will for?"

In Joshua 24, Joshua is leading his people to possess their Promised Land, but they become weary in battle, giving in to compromise. Joshua is fed up. He says:

> "If it seems evil to you to serve the LORD, choose for yourselves this day whom you will serve, whether the gods which your fathers served that were on the other side of the River, or the gods of the Amorites, in whose land you dwell. But as for me and my house, we will serve the Lord."
>
> Joshua 24:15

You can choose to be sick or poor, to serve money or man, but as for me and my house, we will serve the Lord. Choose healing, prosperity, righteousness, and holiness. Refuse to allow anyone authority over your will. "As for me and my house, we will serve the Lord." It's your choice.

The Word Will Change Your Root System

You don't have to be poor, but you'll stay poor if you don't choose to dig the roots of poverty out of your heart and replace them with the truth of God's Word.

You do not have to experience cancer. You can live a long and satisfied life if you choose to put the Word down on the inside of you. (1 John 1:1.) You do not have to go through divorce, but divorce can happen if you do not choose to fill your heart with the Word. The truth will allow your marriage to last.

The right choices will bring the right treasures to your heart, which will produce more right choices and blessings in your life. Even if you are a Christian—born of God, filled with the Spirit of God—old roots of bitterness, jealousy, envy, and anger will produce the same problems the world has. But when you choose to put the Word in your heart, it will show you answers for your marriage and children. You can grow a bountiful crop of the right fruit. Choose well.

If you have time to read a computer manual, the newspaper, and trade magazines, you have time for the Bible. If your company sends you to school for eight weeks, and you can do your best every day in class so you can make another dollar an hour, then you have time to read your Bible.

The Word Prunes You

Jeremiah 1:9-10 says, "Then the Lord put forth His hand and touched my mouth, and the Lord said to me: 'Behold, I have put My words in your mouth. See, I have this day set you over the nations and over the kingdoms, to root out and to pull down, to destroy and to throw down, to build and to plant.'"

The Word of God is what prunes you. The seed grows the abundant life in your heart. "You are already clean because of the word which I have spoken to you" (John 15:3).

Sometimes it is necessary to dig out the roots before you can plant. Sometimes you must pull down before you can build up. When the process of pulling down roots is going on, sometimes you feel like quitting because it seems so difficult. When the process of throwing down is going on, sometimes you feel like throwing up. But don't quit, don't run, don't avoid, don't deny, don't ignore. Let those bad roots come out.

Choose to dig the junk out and build something great. You are created in God's image and have been given the right to choose. Every positive choice strengthens your heart. You have a powerful will that will decide your eternity and, to a great degree, your life on earth. Choose wisely.

Questions

1. What choices have you made that you later regretted and wanted to blame on someone else? (Luke 10:38-42.)

2. When have you used your will to do something that everyone around you disagreed with?

3. What caused you to choose life when you chose God? (Deut. 30:19.)

4. What choices are before you now that would allow your life to be more in line with God's will?

5. Besides you and God, who can cause you to succeed or fail?

6

❦

Guard Your Heart

Once you become aware of the condition of your heart, renew your mind, and choose the good God has for you, it's time to protect the good things growing in your heart.

In Scripture, the Lord compares your heart to a garden. (Jer. 31:12.) In one parable, Jesus says your heart is like soil; if you plant the right seeds, you will bring forth good fruit—some thirty, some sixty, and some a hundredfold. (Matt. 13:23.) Different people will produce different levels of fruit in their lives.

The seed is always the same—it is the Word—but the condition of your heart determines how much you produce. Some hearts are hard, stony ground. Some are shallow and look good for a little while, but don't last. In Matthew 15:13, Jesus says, "…Every plant which My heavenly Father has not planted will be uprooted."

Your goal should be for the garden of your heart to be so healthy that it can grow more fruit. It should produce good results so your lifestyle improves and brings glory to God.

We are to guard our hearts from old thoughts, feelings, and behaviors we know have been a problem. Proverbs 4:23 says, "Keep [or guard] your heart with all diligence, for out of it spring the issues of life."

Protect your heart from the temptation to fall back into your old nature. If you were previously a club dancer, do not conduct business meetings at a club. If you are recovering from alcohol abuse, do not invite someone to meet you at the bar. Stay away from those temptations, and guard your heart. Protect yourself from habits of your old nature.

When I was a child, we had a pasture with some bad seed in it. A certain weed would grow up to five or six feet tall. It was poisonous to the horses, ugly, and fast growing. It choked out the grass and other things we wanted to grow. We cut it down one year with big sickles, piled it up, and burned it. The next spring, it all came back. It spread like wildfire, so my parents told my brother and me to pull it up by the roots.

I discovered that when you pull things up from the roots, it is messy and not much fun. It disturbs the soil and leaves big holes in the ground for a while. When you jerk the roots out, dust goes everywhere. However, when you pull them up by the roots, the weeds do not come back.

Uprooting that which God did not plant is critical to protecting the garden of your heart and maintaining a healthy heart.

A man in our church has a lovely rose garden. He is very particular about the quality and growth of his roses. When weeds begin to grow among his flowers, he yanks them out because he desires quality in the flowers he grows. He gets the weeds out as soon as they show up. That is the only way to keep his roses healthy and to protect them from invaders.

As you dig around in your garden, you may discover plants that were not put there by God. If you ignore the weeds in your garden, they will grow more. Ignorance doesn't solve the problem. It just means you have chosen to allow the weeds in your garden to grow and increase.

Sometimes when we go to church, we do not want anyone to see our weeds. We want to look good. We want to be blessed, happy, healed, and have no problems. So we try to keep up an image and avoid dealing with the problems in our life.

I've had people tell me, "Pastor Treat, I actually felt better about myself before I started coming to Christian Faith Center. I used to be a happy person until I started listening to you. You brought up all these issues, and now I have to face problems I've ignored for years."

Heart Condition and Productivity

In Mark 4:3 Jesus says, "Listen! Behold, a sower went out to sow." Jesus continues in verses 14-15, "The sower sows the word. And these are the ones by the wayside where the word is sown. When they hear, Satan comes immediately and takes away the word that was sown in their hearts." The field represents the heart, and the Word is the seed.

"These likewise are the ones sown on stony ground who, when they hear the word, immediately receive it with gladness;

"and they have no root in themselves, and so endure only for a time. Afterward, when tribulation or persecution arises for the word's sake, immediately they stumble.

"Now these are the ones sown among thorns; they are the ones who hear the word,

"and the cares of this world, the deceitfulness of riches, and the desire for other things entering in choke the word, and it becomes unfruitful.

"But these are the ones sown on good ground, those who hear the word, accept it, and bear fruit: some thirtyfold, some sixty, and some a hundred."

Mark 4:16-20

The seed that falls by the wayside represents people who come to church occasionally. They are on the wayside. They are like the soil on the edge of the field. The sprinkler doesn't quite reach that far, and neither does the fertilizer. A little seed is spread on that soil, but it falls outside the area that receives the care.

Many Christians are still on the wayside. They are not in church enough to be watered and fertilized. They catch a little bit of the seed, but Satan comes immediately and steals away the Word that has been sown in their hearts. The seed cannot grow because they are on the wayside. As soon as they hear something from God, they are too far out to keep it; therefore, that Word is snatched away.

The seed is the same for those considered stony ground, but the heart is different. When they hear the Word, they immediately receive it with gladness, but they have no root in themselves. They are shallow and endure only for a time. Afterward, when tribulation, persecution for the Word's sake, the pressures, challenges, or difficulties of life arise, the shallow heart soil gives up the seed. Jesus called it "stony ground."

They are all fired up about God one day, and the next day they're not sure they're saved. One day they love their church, and the next day they move to a different church. Their hearts have no depth.

With stony ground there's a little bit of earth but a whole lot of hard rock. The seed can't grow, so it quickly springs up but lives a short life. Stony ground represents those who are all excited about the Lord for a little while, but their excitement does not last. Their

Christianity is like a roller coaster, up and down. They are fired up about God and then back in the world. They recommit and rededicate, but they return to their old lifestyle. It is a result of the condition of the heart. The seed is there, but roots cannot be established.

The Word sown among thorns represents people hearing the Word and coming to church now and then, but the soil of their hearts is not prepared. Again, the cares of the world, the deceitfulness of riches, and desire for other things choke out the Word until it becomes unfruitful. These people receive the Word and start out well, but then don't have time for church because their business is prospering, they are traveling, they have a new boat, they are off to play for the weekend. They are busy and have things to do.

The lust for other things and the deceitfulness of riches remove them from all that blessed their lives. Soon they become unfruitful. We later hear that they are divorced and sick and their children have lost their Christian influence. There is no fruit of the Word in their lives.

Satan, persecution, and tribulation come to steal the Word. The lust of other things and the deceitfulness of riches choke the Word.

It is the seed of God's Word in your life that makes a fruitful, productive garden. You may love the Lord; however, the important question is *What is going on with the Word in your life?* If the Word is not big in your heart but is overshadowed by other issues, then your life will not bear fruit. Your heart must be whole in order for you to live a successful life.

People who receive the Word and embrace it are good, fertile ground. We need to be honest with ourselves. Are we producing and improving? Are we increasing thirty, sixty, a hundredfold? If you receive the Word, you will experience results, positive changes, and forward motion in your life.

Is there any progress in your marriage or health? Are you moving forward in your financial giving to the kingdom of God? If there is no increase or improvement, the Word is not growing in your heart. That is not meant to be condemning but to emphasize the importance of recognizing any problems in the garden of your heart. Someone sowed some weeds, and we have to get the rototiller out and break up the hard ground. We've got to do something if the garden isn't producing.

If you are honest with yourself, the issues of your heart will come clean. When you were saved, you began to learn, grow, and change. Negative behaviors fell from you like rotten cherries from a tree. Your life became better, and you were excited about the Lord. Is that still happening today? Is there a thirty, sixty, hundredfold improvement in your life? Maybe not in every area of your life, but somewhere you should be making progress. Check the garden of your heart, and see which areas need change and protection.

The level of the productivity of your life is dependent on the condition of your heart. What kind of harvest are you experiencing? Do you have a "barely-getting-by, just-enough-to-pay-the-bills" garden? Is it a survival garden or a garden of abundance? It depends on the condition of your heart.

Before a gardener can plant, he must prepare the soil. Likewise, we need to protect the soil of our garden through preparation. The Bible says that some hearts are hard. The Old Testament calls such hard, crusty soil "fallow ground." (Jer. 4:3.) A person with a hard heart hears the Word and says, "Yeah, but that doesn't apply to me; I don't like it; I don't believe that; I don't want to hear that; I don't need to listen." Such a person rejects the Word, excuses himself, brushes it off, and goes on about his business. This is dangerous behavior to the garden of a person's heart.

In contrast, when the ground of your garden is soft, the seed will go in and weeds will easily come out. The blessings of God will come up thirty, sixty, and a hundredfold.

Does Your Garden Belong to God?

You cannot walk with God and experience all that God has for you when you only permit God access to certain areas of your garden. He needs unrestricted access to properly help your garden grow.

In Matthew 22:36 Jesus is asked, "Teacher, which is the great commandment in the law?" In verse 37 Jesus says to him, "'...You shall love the Lord your God with all your heart, with all your soul, and with all your mind.'" You cannot love the Lord with half of your heart. You have to love Him with all of your heart. Then He clarifies it. He means with all of your soul—all of your mind, will, and emotions. Remember, your will and your mind are your thoughts and attitudes.

When the world around you begins to fall, look to see what your garden produces. If you have guarded your heart, you will find healing for your family, salvation for your children, and direction for your future. Gain this understanding now so you don't have to say, "I wish I would have...." You can save yourself a trip to the penitentiary, the hospital, the courtroom, or the lawyer's office. It is time to be wholehearted about the things of God.

God's will for healing, blessing, health, and wholeness is the same for everyone, but the condition of your heart determines what you can grow in your life. The Word is the seed, and it is always good, alive, and able to produce, but there are different kinds of heart soil.

Many people say, "Whatever the Lord wills," or, "If God wants it to happen...." No. The seed of the Word is always the same. Stay with the Word; believe and speak it.

The Pruning Process

In John 15:1 Jesus says, "I am the true vine, and My Father is the vinedresser [or the gardener]." Some translations say, "My Father is the gardener. He takes care of the plants."

> "Every branch in Me that does not bear fruit He takes away; and every branch that bears fruit He prunes, that it may bear more fruit."
>
> John 15:2

The Lord wants everyone in the body of Christ to produce results and bear fruit.[1] If you do nothing in the kingdom, you will be cut off.[2] Jesus said it in the Bible. If you are bearing fruit, He will prune you so you can produce more fruit.

> "You are already clean because of the word which I have spoken to you."
>
> John 15:3

"Clean" in this verse is the Greek word that "pruned" is derived from in verse 2.[3] So you could say, "You are already pruned because of the Word which I have spoken to you."

When you hear about God pruning lives, you may think of sermons about how God gave you cancer to make you more spiritual, God wrecked your car to see if you really trusted Him, God took away your family to see who was first in your life—God pruning you through disasters and problems. Those are religious interpretations of God's pruning and not true.

The Scripture makes clear God's pruning process. "You are already clean [pruned] because of the word which I have spoken to you.... If you abide in Me, and My words abide in you, you will ask what you desire, and it shall be done for you" (John 15:3,7).

If you have unfulfilled desires, ask yourself, "Am I abiding in Jesus, and are His words living in me?" If you have dreams and desires that have not been fulfilled, check the soil of your heart. When the Word works in your heart, you can "ask what you desire, and it shall be done for you" (John 15:7). If His Word is in your heart, you will not ask anything that contradicts His will.

The Word of God is a vital part of a healed, healthy, strong heart. Many Christians do not read the Bible. They love the Lord and go to church but do not study to know what the Bible says for their lives. Consistent input of the Word is necessary for a whole heart. The Word is the seed that grows a good garden.

Protect your heart. Make it a garden of health, wholeness, and productivity for God's kingdom. Weed out the things that were not planted by God. Water your garden with the Word of God, and see God's blessings overtake your life. Jesus said, "'...Man shall not live by bread alone, but by every Word that proceeds from the mouth of God'" (Matt. 4:4). And according to Psalm 107:20, "He sent His Word and healed them. . . ."

Questions

1. Based on the fruit from the garden of your heart up to this point in your life, how would you rate the soil of your life? (Mark 4:20.)

2. What thoughts, attitudes, or beliefs do you see as weeds or hindrances to cultivating a healthy garden in your heart?

3. How are you putting the Word of God into the garden of your heart to uproot and replace weeds? (Mark 4:14.)

7

The Right Confession

When I say the word "confess" or "confession," many people immediately think of confessing sin. That's only half of the process. A healthy heart confesses faults to remove what is wrong and confesses the Word of God to receive what is right. In Mark 11:23 Jesus said that you will have whatever you say.

We don't confess sin to someone so that God will forgive us. God forgives us when we confess our faults to Him: "…He is faithful and just to forgive us our sins and to cleanse us from all unrighteousness" (1 John 1:9).

James said, "Confess your faults one to another, and pray one for another, that ye may be healed…" (James 5:16 KJV). We confess our pains, problems, and challenges to other strong Christians who will pray and agree with us for a whole heart.

We confess not only to get right with God, but also to get right with ourselves.

I have sat down with the ministry staff and said, "Here is what I am going through. People are getting divorced, a pastor from another church is involved in adultery, and I am frustrated and upset. I am asking you to pray with me so I can deal with these things correctly and do not become depressed or angry."

Each of us reacts to circumstances in different ways, but when we confess a negative attitude or a sin, we are free from it. If we refuse to confess our sins, we are bound to those sins. You don't want your children to get away with lying because you're concerned with being labeled a mean parent. If your children get away with it, they begin to build a lifestyle of lying and become bound to that sin. We are free from what we confess and bound to what we cover.

Someone recently came to me and said, "Pastor, I made a mistake. I became involved with a girl who was not right for me. I can't believe I did it, but I need to share my situation with you." He did not need to talk to me so God would forgive him. God forgave him when he confessed it to Him, but he confessed it to me for healing and restoration. It was his step toward a healthy heart.

If you have a problem with pornography, go to a Christian who is strong and mature in the things of the Lord and confess it. You will be free to move forward and overcome that negative behavior.

Confessing faults is only half of the process toward having a whole heart. On the positive side, we confess what we believe and reach for. Jesus said:

> "For assuredly, I say to you, whoever says to this mountain, 'Be removed and be cast into the sea,' and does not doubt in his heart, but believes that those things he says will come to pass, he will have whatever he says."
>
> Mark 11:23

James chapter three teaches us that our tongue can release heaven and blessing or hell and cursing in our lives. We must speak positive, godly, and scriptural things to receive them in our lives. Much of Israel died in a wilderness because of their murmuring, unbelief, and negative confessions. (Num. 14:31-34.)

Forgetting and Forgiving the Past

In Philippians 3, Paul talked about his heritage—his background, education, degrees, and position in society. He said, "...If anyone else thinks he may have confidence in the flesh, I more so" (Phil. 3:4). Then he released all of his fleshly accomplishments and essentially called them "dung" (v. 8 KJV), manure, "rubbish":

> Circumcised the eighth day, of the stock of Israel, of the tribe of Benjamin, a Hebrew of the Hebrews; concerning the law, a Pharisee;
>
> Concerning zeal, persecuting the church; concerning righteousness which is in the law, blameless.
>
> But what things were gain to me, these I have counted loss for Christ.
>
> Yet indeed I also count all things loss for the excellence of the knowledge of Christ Jesus my Lord, for whom I have suffered the loss of all things, and count them as rubbish, that I may gain Christ.
>
> Philippians 3:5-8

You must release the past to live in peace and joy. That includes the bad and the good. Paul said, "I was successful in the world. I was at the top. I was king of the mountain." In the Jewish world, he was number one. In the Sanhedrin, there was great respect for this young man, who at that time was called Saul of Tarsus.

He said in effect, "I could be puffed up, feeling good over what I did back then, my degrees, my college experience, my position in society, but I count it all as rubbish. I let it go and leave it behind."

Then in verses 12-15 Paul says:

> Not that I have already attained, or am already perfected; but I press on, that I may lay hold of that for which Christ Jesus has also laid hold of me.
>
> Brethren, I do not count myself to have apprehended; but one thing I do, forgetting those things which are behind and reaching forward to those things which are ahead,
>
> I press toward the goal for the prize of the upward call of God in Christ Jesus. Therefore let us, as many as are mature, have this mind; and if in anything you think otherwise, God will reveal even this to you.

We must forget what is behind, and press on. The windshield is bigger than the rearview mirror. The view looking back is never as clear as the view looking forward. That is why you will often find a little sign on rearview mirrors that say something like "Objects may appear different than they really are."

Someone who won a national championship in 1971 and continually shares it as his primary focus in life needs to stick the trophy in the attic and move on with life. Forget those things which are behind, and press on.

Around football season, some guys relive their football days of thirty years ago. If the exciting days are yesterdays, you cannot experience peace and joy. If your memories are more invigorating than your visions, you live in the past. Peace and joy come from the kingdom, and the kingdom is not about yesterday. It is about today and tomorrow. A healthy heart looks forward to the promises to come.

Paul not only experienced the good in his past; he also experienced the bad. Until he became a Christian, he locked Christians in jail and killed them. He participated in stoning to death great men like the deacon Stephen.

At the end of his life, though, Paul said that he had, "wronged no man" (2 Cor. 7:2). He could say that because he had confessed and released his past. He had received forgiveness. He became a new creature in Christ and was renewed each day.

As a member of the Sanhedrin, Paul must have been married. Possibly he had children. But he called himself single as an apostle.[1] (1 Cor. 7:8 AMP.) So did his wife die, or did she leave him? Did his children die or leave him? He lived as a single man. He said, "…one thing I do, forgetting those things which are behind…."

We cannot live with what we used to be. We can only live with what we are and what we are to become.

> …forgetting those things which are behind and reaching forward to those things which are ahead,
>
> I press toward the goal for the prize of the upward call of God in Christ Jesus.
>
> Philippians 3:13,14

Olympic athletes press for the finish line. Often, that last little strain makes the difference between a winner and second place.

If you're in the midst of a workout and your mind reverts to something from your past that was a real bummer and for some reason you get stuck on this negative thought, your strength diminishes.

An athlete nearing the finish line is not thinking about last year's failure or injury. Likewise, someone winning the race of life is pressing for the prize of the high calling of God, which is ahead, not behind. Paul said that a successful future requires the ability to release the good and the bad from your past.

Forgive

In Matthew 6:12, in what is known as the Lord's Prayer, Jesus says, "And forgive us our debts, as we forgive our debtors." Jesus put into this prayer the concept that we are to forgive even before difficulty arises. If we prayed this prayer and made it our lifestyle every morning, before anything happened, we would forgive. We would decide we were not going to be hurt or angry. We would refuse to hold grudges but would forgive, even as God has forgiven us.

Jesus had more to say about forgiveness in verses 14-15:

"For if you forgive men their trespasses, your heavenly Father will also forgive you.

"But if you do not forgive men their trespasses, neither will your Father forgive your trespasses."

Your relationship with God and the openness you have with Him depend on your ability to forgive people. If you hold anything against anyone, you have shut the door between you and God. You have caused pain and hurt to your heart. God has already forgiven you, but you cannot receive it.

You feel this separation between you and God and do not understand, or you may not even be conscious of it. There is just a feeling like the Lord is out there somewhere instead of close and intimate. An unwillingness to forgive will cause you to lose the sense of God's Presence.

When you are frustrated with people and angry about things that have happened to you, your feelings close you off to the Lord. You must forgive men their trespasses in order to receive the Father's forgiveness. The only way to open the relationship with the Lord is to release your negative feelings against people.

Often we do not understand what forgiveness is. We confuse forgiveness with restoration and trust. There are people I have forgiven, but I don't trust them. If a person steals your belongings, you forgive him and you let it go. That doesn't mean you put him in charge of your finances.

We may mistakenly think forgiveness is restoration or trust. Forgiveness means "I'm not holding anything against you. I release it. I'm not angry, mad, hurt, or upset over the situation." You may have some things you need to deal with, but forgive and release the one who hurt you.

In Mark 11:25 Jesus says, "And whenever you stand praying, if you have anything against anyone, forgive him, that your Father in heaven may also forgive you your trespasses."

Even if you think the person does not deserve forgiveness, Jesus says, "Forgive him." The Lord didn't talk about what that person should do; He talked about what *you* should do. You may think, *He deserves to die,* but God tells you to forgive him. Maybe this person has not asked for forgiveness. The Lord did not tell you to wait for him to ask. He said, "Forgive him."

How long can you stand praying? You do not have much time to hold things against people. Maybe you have held things against people for so long that you cannot even remember what you were holding against them. Confess your unwillingness to forgive, and then forgive them.

Forgive Yourself

The Lord said, "Whenever you stand praying, if you have anything against anyone, forgive him...." That includes you, too. Sometimes we hold things against ourselves: "How could I do that?" "Why was I so stupid?" "I let my marriage fail." "I lost that job." "How could I?"

While you "stand praying," you may be mad at yourself, but when you finish praying, let it go. Forgive yourself. Put your hand over your heart and say, "I forgive myself."

Forgiveness Is a Choice

Forgiveness is not a "feeling" that comes and goes. It's not something that some people can do but others can't. It is a command from God, which means you *can* forgive. Forgiveness is a choice. It is your decision.

You can say, "You lied to me, and you hurt my feelings, but I forgive."

How do you feel about it? You may feel mad, frustrated, hurt. But once you forgive and memories of the situation come back, remind yourself, "I forgave and let that go." It may come back numerous times, but each time the thought comes into your mind, follow your decision with the thought, *I forgave. I let it go.* Thoughts produce feelings. Eventually you will feel differently. Remember, we renew our minds. You will no longer have the anger, anxiety, bitterness, or frustration.

Many of us have been upset and angry for so long that it has changed our personality. We have become critical, cynical, suspicious, and angry. You may not even know the real you anymore.

You deserve to be free. You deserve to let go of that offense. Refuse to live with that pain any longer. Choose to forgive. Make your thoughts follow your decision to forgive. The feelings will follow.

Know When To Confront

In Luke 17:3-4 Jesus says:

"Take heed to yourselves. If your brother sins against you, rebuke him; and if he repents, forgive him.

"And if he sins against you seven times in a day, and seven times in a day returns to you, saying, 'I repent,' you shall forgive him."

"Rebuke him" means to confront the issue.[2]

However, Mark 11:25 implies that there are times when you don't need to talk to the person and confront the issue. You just need to say, "I'm done with this. I release it. I forgive, and let's go on with our business."

There are other situations in which you will not be able to improve the circumstance, so you just let it go. You have to decide what is best. If the person is unaware of what you have been hurt or angry about, do not make him aware.

I have people come up to me regularly who say, "Pastor, I want to ask you to forgive me." I always say, "I forgive you." They say, "You don't even know what I did."

"I don't want to know. Whatever you did, I choose to forgive you."

"But I just wanted you to know, I've hated you for six months."

"I thought we were friends."

"I told everybody that you are demon-possessed." Or "I wrote a book about you and said your church is a cult."

That information gives me a whole lot to forgive. I have already decided to forgive, but now it will take some work.

I am not talking about hiding things from people who are close to you. I am not talking about lying to cover up. But in the area of forgiveness, when you release things, let them go. If you need to discuss it or confront it, then do so; then let it go.

Forgiveness Sets People Free

Luke 17:5 says, "And the apostles said to the Lord, 'Increase our faith.'" They realized that forgiveness is not easy. It is a lifestyle principle that we do not carry the hurts and pains of other people. It is a choice to forgive, and it takes faith to move on.

In John 20:23 Jesus says, "If you forgive the sins of any, they are forgiven them; if you retain the sins of any, they are retained." There are cases in which your forgiveness actually sets the other person free. We must decide to be free and to free others by not holding grudges, gossiping, being angry, or being hurt.

In Ephesians 4:32 Paul says, "Be kind to one another, tenderhearted, forgiving one another, just as God in Christ forgave you."

In Matthew 18 Jesus tells of a man who has been forgiven of a debt of $10 million, in modern financial terms.[3] Then he walks right out of the courtroom where he has been forgiven and holds a friend in bondage over a twenty-dollar debt. When the judge finds out, he has the first man thrown into prison and turned over to the tormentors. The judge says to him:

"'You wicked servant! I forgave you all that debt because you begged me.

'Should you not also have had compassion on your fellow servant, just as I had pity on you?'

"And his master was angry, and delivered him to the torturers until he should pay all that was due him."

Matthew 18:32-34

In Romans 12:19 Paul says, "Beloved, do not avenge yourselves, but rather give place to wrath; for it is written, 'Vengeance is Mine, I will repay,' says the Lord."

Your job is to take heed to yourself and keep yourself free. Keep your heart open through confessing what is right and what is wrong. Forgive yourself. Do not stay mad at yourself or anyone else.

Let Go of the Low Life

God designed you to live an abundant life. If you lose the low life, you find the high life. (Matt. 10:39 AMP.) Sometimes we hang on to the low life for all the wrong reasons.

It can be compared to the little boy with the blanket that wore out a year ago. He does not want to let go of it. It is too small and no longer will keep him warm. It does not look pretty, as it did when Grandma first gave it to him, but he hangs on to it because it is *his* blanket.

You may be hanging on to a job that is not your destiny, because you are comfortable. When you are secure and mature in the Lord and you realize who you are in Christ, you can leave that old position and move on to God's best for your life.

Your life is not restricted by God, Satan, your boss, or your spouse. You are limited not by circumstances but by what's in your own heart.

The Message Bible translation of 2 Corinthians 6:11-12 reads:

> Dear, dear Corinthians, I can't tell you how much I long for you to enter this wide-open, spacious life. We didn't fence you in. The smallness you feel comes from within you. Your lives aren't small, but you're living them in a small way.

Quit talking about what you wish you could do but probably never will, what you'd like to do but can't afford, what you'd like to give but aren't able to, and what you'd like to accomplish but probably won't. Remove the restrictions and limitations. Paul said, "Your lives aren't small, but you live them in small ways." Confess what the Word says can happen in your life.

The smallness comes not because of circumstances, but because of what's in your heart. We often allow our hearts to pick up, carry, and hold the hurts, failures, difficulties, and tragedies of our past.

In various ways we're all victims of accidents and circumstances, but we must make sure that we don't become victims for life. Move on. In the words of the apostle Paul, "Forget what is behind and press on."

However, you cannot get over it by one touch, by one supernatural miracle, or by a quantum leap into the Spirit. Second Corinthians 7:1 says, "...let us cleanse ourselves from all filthiness of the flesh and spirit, perfecting holiness in the fear of God." We must be cleansed from that which defiles and distracts us within and without.

To have a healed heart, you have to believe it is possible to live without fear, lay your head down, go to sleep, and wake up eight hours later. That would be a miracle for some. It is possible: "Jesus said unto him, If thou canst believe, all things are possible to him that believeth" (Mark 9:23 KJV).

It is possible to have the marriage you have dreamed of. It is possible to live without debt and be free of financial worries. It is possible to live for years without any illness.

How do you do it? Follow these four steps:

1. **Release everything you cannot change.** We spend so much time talking about things we cannot change. You do not have energy to think about, talk about, look at, or deal with anything you cannot change. If it cannot be changed, don't think about it.

2. **Take steps of change.** "I'm just waiting for a breakthrough" is a classic excuse. You'd better take a step, because your breakthrough may be five years away. You are not going to lose twenty pounds tomorrow, but you could lose one-quarter of a pound today.

3. **Confess the right things into your heart by staying close to the Holy Spirit.** The world will push you toward things that keep you sick. If you are not close to the Holy Spirit, you will pick up that spirit of the world. The church is

experiencing the same failures as the world is because we stay closer to the world than we do to the Holy Spirit.

4. **Pray in the Holy Spirit every day.** When you get up in the morning, start your day praying in the Spirit. You have a few things on your agenda. You don't have all the answers for every circumstance, but the Holy Spirit does. He will give you answers and ideas, whether they are for a business appointment or for dealing with your children.

As you pray in the Holy Spirit, your inner man will be built up. You need to strengthen your inner man, build up your spirit and your soul.

Praying in the Holy Spirit edifies the inner person. It refreshes your inner man. First Corinthians 14:4 says, "He who speaks in a tongue edifies himself...."

As you pray in the Holy Spirit, you will receive revelation knowledge. Before you enter the same argument you have had with your spouse for the last twelve years, let the Holy Spirit guide you. As long as you are listening to yourself instead of the Spirit of God, you will repeat the same behaviors. The Holy Spirit will show you areas to confess and change as well as areas to pursue for a successful life.

Living Water From the Inside Out

Jesus says in John 7:38 KJV, "...out of his belly shall flow rivers of living water." That living water is healing, peace, joy, love, relationships, prosperity, and creativity. It is a happy, abundant life.

God has already given you abundant life, but you must let it flow through your spirit and your soul so the kingdom of God can be manifested.

> Therefore we do not lose heart. Even though our outward man is perishing, yet the inward man is being renewed day by day.
>
> 2 Corinthians 4:16

Notice the outward and inward man. We tend to focus on the outward and think that if we could make the outward look right or feel right, everything would be okay. Paul says, "The outward man is perishing."

We need the living water to flow, and we need to receive the refreshing of the Holy Spirit so the righteousness, peace, and joy of the Holy Spirit can rule and reign in our hearts.

Let's follow Scripture and confess our faults as well as what we want to receive from the Lord. Let's confess increase in our income, blessing on our kids, a great future for our family, changes and improvements in our company or whatever we are involved with. Confession plays a powerful part in receiving a whole heart.

Questions

1. Are there some things you need to confess to the Lord or to others to cleanse your heart?

2. Are there some things you should forgive yourself for?

3. Are you looking back to the past for fulfillment? Confess the dreams you have for the future.

4. Do you spend time edifying and building up your inner man by praying in the Holy Spirit?

8

❦

Keeping Godly Focus and Vision

Someone once said, "What you see is what you get." Colossians 3:2 says, "Set your mind on things above, not on things on the earth." I interpret this to mean that we are to think not only *about* heaven, but *as* heaven thinks. If you will focus on the things of God, you will prosper and experience success in every area of your life.

Psalm 1:1-3 says:

Blessed is the man who walks not in the counsel of the ungodly, nor stands in the path of sinners, nor sits in the seat of the scornful;

But his delight is in the law of the Lord, and in His law he meditates day and night.

He shall be like a tree planted by the rivers of water, that brings forth its fruit in its season, whose leaf also shall not wither; and whatever he does shall prosper.

Proverbs 3:5-8 says:

Trust in the Lord with all your heart, and lean not on your own understanding;

In all your ways acknowledge Him, and He shall direct your paths.

Do not be wise in your own eyes; fear the Lord and depart from evil.

It will be health to your flesh, and strength to your bones.

Notice the phrase "all your heart." Why didn't the Scripture say, "Trust the Lord with your heart"? Instead, it specifies "*all* your heart."

We can easily be halfhearted in our walk with God. We trust God for some things but not for all things.

We trust the Lord when it comes to eternity and our salvation, but when it comes to our marriage, we keep that under our control. In other words, we do not follow God's Word and will in marriage because of our lack of trust for God to do what He has promised.

We do not trust the Lord fully when it comes to our children. We follow the latest pop psychology, or what the public school says. We should teach our children how to focus their thoughts on the ways of God. You cannot protect your children from all the evil influences of the world, but you can teach them how to respond to the evils of the world. Instead of being so concerned that your children might overhear a cuss word on television or in the movies, focus their thoughts on what is good and right according to the Word of God.

Marriage and children are just a couple of issues that many people do not fully trust God with. I am convinced that there are many Christians who love God, are good people, and are headed to heaven, but do not fully trust God with *all* of their heart. When it comes to our finances, for example, we trust the banker, but we do not trust the Lord with *all* of our heart. We aren't focused on His thoughts and His ways. We reserve certain areas of our lives to do it our way instead of God's way because we do not share His perspective.

A Pharisee asked Jesus, "'Teacher, which is the great commandment in the law?' Jesus said to him, 'You shall love the Lord your God with all your heart, with all your soul, and with all your mind'" (Matt. 22:36,37).

Jesus emphasized "with *all* your heart, with *all* your soul, and with *all* your mind." It's important to realize that when we love God with all of our heart, that includes loving Him with all of our soul and with all of our mind. It takes every part of our heart to obtain His way of doing things. A healthy, whole heart focuses on the thoughts and ways of God.

Joshua 1:8 says:

This Book of the Law shall not depart from your mouth, but you shall meditate in it day and night, that you may observe to do according to all that is written in it. For then you will make your way prosperous, and then you will have good success.

Strive for a place where your heart is whole so you can trust God with all your heart and commit to Him. Then you can discover His thoughts, intents, and purposes for a successful life that is pleasing to God.

God tells us in Isaiah 55:9, "For as the heavens are higher than the earth, so are My ways higher than your ways, and My thoughts than your thoughts." It is time to come up to His perspective.

Wholly Focused on Him

God desires to see us focused on Him through trust. If you are focused on things of the world, your heart is not focused on Him. The Bible says that you cannot love the Father and the world. (Luke 16:13.) To love the world is enmity against God. (James 4:4.) To love the world and to love God at the same time is to live a half-hearted, schizophrenic lifestyle.

At one time or another most of us have said, "I really want to live like a Christian, but I am attracted to these other things." All of us have thoughts and desires. If our hearts are wholly focused on the Lord, then we can quickly reject the things of the world and stay connected to what God has for our lives.

Distractions can toss you back and forth. Get serious about a healed, whole heart. Focus on Him, and trust Him with all that you are.

If any of you lacks wisdom, let him ask of God, who gives to all liberally and without reproach, and it will be given to him.

But let him ask in faith, with no doubting, for he who doubts is like a wave of the sea driven and tossed by the wind.

James 1:5,6

When you doubt, you may want to believe but aren't sure. You say you have faith but also have doubts. Doubts are signs that you are not driven by the Word and will of God. You are driven by circumstances and tossed by the wind. Other things control your life.

For let not that man *[that person who doubts, wavers, or trusts God with less than all of his heart]* suppose that he will receive anything from the Lord;

he is a double-minded man, unstable in all his ways.

James 1:7,8

At times all of us have thoughts that are not of God, and we have to reject them. But there's a difference between a thought and a lifestyle.

For example, say something happens on your job. You become angry and think, *I'd like to tell him off.* You quickly realize that's not going to help, so you make a decision to go on about your business. That is a positive lifestyle decision focused on peace.

However, if you continue to think contrarily to God's way, you become double-minded. Maybe you say you want to serve God, but you continue to do things the way the world does them. You say you trust God, but you continue to do things the way the world does, perhaps through business deals that lack integrity.

James says, "Don't even think that you will receive anything from the Lord. A double-minded person is unstable." If you cannot love God with all of your heart, you are unstable and God cannot provide for you the things He wants you to have.

I love Wendy with all of my heart. I can't say, "My heart is so big that I could love two or three women." Wendy would say, "No, I don't think so." In terms of marital love, my heart is wholly hers.

Likewise, I cannot say, "My heart is so big that I could serve God and the world." It just doesn't work. In our society, it is lauded as admirable when you embrace opposing beliefs. For example, you believe that abortion is wrong, but you would never want to tell someone else because you would not want to pass laws to hinder her from having an abortion. That is a double-minded person. You have somehow embraced opposing beliefs. If your heart is toward God, you will respect life. You will guard the sanctity, holiness, and value of life.

We have the ability to compartmentalize our heart. Some of these compartments oppose each other. Society calls it being broad-minded, but the Bible says it is confusion. There is no focus or commitment. You can say "I do" at the altar, but what you really mean is "I'll try." You say, "Until death do us part," but what you mean is "Until I'm fed up with you." We compartmentalize, and our heart grows unhealthy.

I believe one of the reasons this happens is that our hearts get hardened. When your heart is hardened, you are not aware of what is going on in your life.

The Pharisees asked Jesus about marriage relationships and why they fail. Jesus said, "...Moses, because of the hardness of your hearts, permitted you to divorce your wives, but from the beginning it was not so" (Matt. 19:8).

Jesus said the reason Moses set up a divorce program was that their hearts were hard. It was not because of personality problems, their calling, or an alternative lifestyle; it was not because they married the wrong person. None of those are valid reasons for divorce, but they are reasons given over and over again in our society today. Our hearts are out of focus.

You Have Control Over Your Own Heart

Jesus says you can make your heart whatever you want it to be. You decide. God gave you sovereignty in your life, sovereignty in the choice of your destiny, and sovereign control over your heart.

> "Either make the tree good and its fruit good, or else make the tree bad and its fruit bad; for a tree is known by its fruit.
>
> "Brood of vipers! How can you, being evil, speak good things? For out of the abundance of the heart the mouth speaks.
>
> "A good man out of the good treasure of his heart brings forth good things, and an evil man out of the evil treasure brings forth evil things."
>
> Matthew 12:33-35

What is in your heart is up to you. Obviously, you can be affected or influenced by the world, but it is still up to you to decide what kind of a heart you want to have and what you want to have in your heart.

In Exodus 3 God tells Moses he is the man to deliver the Israelites out of Egypt and "set My people free."

Moses is not excited; he says, "No way, Lord. I can't do it. I don't talk very good. I'm not very smart. I'm not eloquent. I stutter." (Ex. 4:10.)

God says, "Moses, you're the one."

Finally God becomes upset with Moses and brings Aaron alongside. (Ex. 4:14-16.) Moses and Aaron go to Pharaoh and, in essence, say, "Pharaoh, we want you to let all your slaves go. No more free labor. We're leaving and moving to a land that God is going to give to us."

Pharaoh says, "No way."

Therefore, they begin the battle, and the plagues start coming down on Egypt. You know how the story goes. In Exodus 7:3-5, God says:

> "I will harden Pharaoh's heart, and multiply My signs and My wonders in the land of Egypt.

"But Pharaoh will not heed you, so that I may lay My hand on Egypt and bring My armies and My people, the children of Israel, out of the land of Egypt by great judgments.

"And the Egyptians shall know that I am the Lord...."

It appears that God hardened Pharaoh's heart. Many of us might believe that God or our environment decides our heart condition; many do not really believe that the condition of our hearts is under our control. But that is the opposite of what Jesus said in Matthew 12:35.

It certainly appears in Pharaoh's case that he did not have any choice. God said, "I will harden Pharaoh's heart...." It seems as if He did this to show the Israelites that He was God. We read this and speculate that if Moses and the Israelites had slipped out of town before the plagues were loosed upon the Egyptians, they never would have known the awesome power of God, because the hard heart of Pharaoh brought all the plagues to pass.

However, the truth of the matter is that carnal, secular mentalities nurtured Pharaoh's heart. God spoke to him, revealed His will and plan, and Pharaoh's heart responded to God in a certain way.

At the same time that God dealt with Pharaoh, God dealt with Moses. Moses' heart was different. Though he struggled along the way, he had a godly mother and was reared with a sense of destiny and knowledge of God. When God called to him on the backside of the desert and began to speak to him, the light of God's Word began to shine on Moses' heart. Moses reacted differently than Pharaoh did because Moses was focused on the thoughts of God.

Moses' heart was like wax. Wax softens as light, sun, and heat are applied. The softened heart can be molded, stretched, and enlarged. It can be adjusted. It is flexible. It does not get hard.

Pharaoh's heart was like clay. Clay becomes hard as the sun begins to shine on it. The more God talked to Pharaoh, the harder his heart became. The more he heard about God's will and God's plan, the harder his heart became.

God's Word and will are the same for all people. The same sun that hardened Pharaoh's heart softened Moses'. The focus of your heart is the controlling factor of how you respond to the light of God's Word. Your attitude, mentality, beliefs, and choices decide whether you grow hard or soft under the bright light of God's Word. You are the one who decides whether you are pliable or callused to the things of God.

Isn't it amazing that when you spank one child, he looks you in the face with a scowl and says, "That didn't hurt," but when you spank another child, he says, "I'm sorry"? They were reared in the same house and have the same parents, the same spirit, and the same environment. What is the difference? Heart choices.

The wind, which lifts one plane higher in the sky, can cause another to crash.

Your attitude determines whether your heart softens or hardens in the presence of God's truth. The light of God's Word, which softens one heart, can have a hardening effect on the heart of the person sitting next to you. You decide; God does not. He hardens the heart if it is already clay, but He softens the heart if it is wax.

At times we develop a hard heart because of what we have been through. We feel as if we have to be hard to stand against the knocks of life. But a hard heart does not make you stronger or tougher. It just breaks much more quickly than a soft heart does. The soft, open, flexible heart "takes a lickin' and keeps on tickin'."

Some people allow their hearts to be hard as a defense mechanism. They think that being hard and tough and keeping their shell intact will enable them to stand against the attacks of the world. Instead, the toughness weakens them and cracks begin to form. The problems of life become harder and harder. The soft heart, however, can absorb the blow, not be affected, and keep right on going in God's will.

Three Tests for a Heart Focused on God

How do you know if your heart is becoming hard? How do you know if you are keeping your heart soft and focused on God? Here are three ways you can check the condition of your heart.

(1) Can You Submit?

Can you submit to God, to people, and to those in authority over you? An immediate sign of a hard heart is problems with authority. Teenagers aren't the only people who have problems with authority. In fact, most teens reflect their perception of what they have seen in their parents.

The teen with problems at school probably has a father who says, "Where's my fuzz-buster? I don't want to obey the law. I just want to make sure I don't get busted by the law." Purchasing equipment to purposefully break the law does not reflect godly character.

If you break the law and get a ticket, you should say, "Thank you, officer. I was breaking the law. I deserve to reap what I have sown. Give me the ticket." Don't make excuses and try to talk your way out of it.

James 4:6-8 says, "He gives more grace...'God resists the proud, but gives grace to the humble.' Therefore submit to God. Resist the devil and he will flee from you. Draw near to God and He will draw near to you. Cleanse your hands, you sinners; and purify your hearts, you double-minded."

If you are double-minded, you cannot focus on God. Trust God with all your heart. Open up to Him with willingness to submit to authority, leadership, and other people.

Submission is evidence of a focused heart. When you resist and become defensive, realize your heart may be hardening toward the things of God.

(2) Do You Have a Desire to Learn?

Psalm 10:17 says, "Lord, You have heard the desire of the humble; You will prepare their heart; You will cause Your ear to hear."

To be humble is to be hungry, open, teachable, and meek. Scripture says Moses was the meekest man on the earth. (Num. 12:3.) Moses called down on Egypt ten of the most horrendous plagues the world has ever known. He split the Red Sea, brought water out of the rock, and had quail meat flown in airmail for a whole nation to feast on. Moses judged tens of thousands of rebellious, stiff-necked Israelites and sent them to a fiery furnace as the earth swallowed them up. Moses had done more than any human being had ever done, and the Lord said, "That's the meekest guy I know."

Moses no longer waited for Aaron to speak up. He had taken the rod of authority and his position with

God. He was focused on God's plan and looking at his life from God's perspective.

Moses' father-in-law, Jethro, asked him, "…What is this thing that you are doing for the people? Why do you alone sit, and all the people stand before you from morning until evening?" (Ex.18:14).

Moses said, "…Because the people come to me to inquire of God. When they have a difficulty, they come to me, and I judge between one and another; and I make known the statutes of God and His laws" (Ex. 18:15,16).

Then Moses' father-in-law said, "…The thing that you do is not good" (Ex. 18:17).

Moses worked for his father-in-law. If I were Moses, I might have asked, "How many sheep do you have on the backside of the desert, Jeth? Thirty-seven sheep? And you are telling me what I am doing is not good? Have you read the newspaper lately? Do you know who wiped out the Egyptian army? Did you see what I can do with this rod?"

It would have been so easy for Moses to brush Jethro off, but Moses listened as Jethro spoke:

"Both you and these people who are with you will surely wear yourselves out. For this thing is too much for you; you are not able to perform it by yourself.

"Listen now to my voice; I will give you counsel, and God will be with you: Stand before God for the people, so that you may bring the difficulties to God.

"And you shall teach them the statutes and the laws, and show them the way in which they must walk and the work they must do.

"Moreover you shall select from all the people able men, such as fear God, men of truth, hating covetousness; and place such over them to be rulers of thousands, rulers of hundreds, rulers of fifties, and rulers of tens.

"And let them judge the people at all times. Then it will be that every great matter they shall bring to you, but every small matter they themselves shall judge. So it will be easier for you, for they will bear the burden with you.

"If you do this thing, and God so commands you, then you will be able to endure, and all this people will also go to their place in peace."

Exodus 18:18-23

Moses did what the guy from the backside of the desert with thirty-seven sheep told him to do. Yet some of us believe we are the greatest thing that's happened since Moses. This is evidence of a hard heart.

I am surprised when I talk to some young person who can barely tie his shoe, whose life is a wreck, but his attitude is "I know everything, and you can't tell me a thing." I'm thinking, *At fourteen, his life is over, because he has no desire to learn.* Do you have a desire to learn, grow, and change?

Jesus said, "...unless you are converted and become as little children, you will by no means enter the kingdom of heaven" (Matt. 18:3).

The greatest attribute of a child is his curiosity and quest for knowledge. Children absorb knowledge like sponges, while many of us act as if we already know. Even when we say we want to learn, it is hard for us because we have an image to uphold. Yet the sign of a soft heart is a hunger for the things of God and a willingness to learn.

(3) Are You Open and Honest?

In 1 John 4:20 Jesus says, "If someone says, 'I love God,' and hates his brother, he is a liar; for he who does not love his brother whom he has seen, how can he love God whom he has not seen?"

Many people use spiritual language to push people away. They might go to someone and say, "The Lord spoke to me, and I'm moving to a different job."

That person may ask, "Why?"

"Because the Lord spoke to me. You have nothing to say about this. Don't even think about giving me your opinion." That kind of talk pushes people away.

It is not smart to isolate yourself and rage against wise judgment. My wife and I don't do anything just because we think God told us to do it. We are constantly requesting input: "What do you think?" "Tell us how you feel." "Does this look good?" "Does it sound like a wise decision?" We often receive better ideas and wise opinions from friends and professionals who have expertise in various areas.

When your heart is soft, you are not afraid to listen and take counsel. You are able to receive. You do not have to act like you know it all.

It's easy to say, "I am open to God, but I am not open to people." Many people who are not hearing from God just say "God told me" so they do not have to deal with people. To say "God told me" can be a defense mechanism. Obviously, the Lord can speak to someone, but when the focus of his life does not improve, you know he did not really hear from God. When God speaks to someone, the fruit is evident.

> A man who isolates himself seeks his own desire; he rages against all wise judgment.
>
> A fool has no delight in understanding, but in expressing his own heart.
>
> Proverbs 18:1,2

Many of us do not talk with our friends. We just make announcements. When you only give announcements, there is no relationship or interaction. It is a sign that your heart is hard.

A few years ago, a couple whom we believed were close friends and who were actively involved in ministry with us approached us after a Sunday night service and asked for a couple minutes to chat. I said, "Sure. Do you want to go get some coffee?"

"No," they replied, "let's just sit back here."

Once we were settled, they said, "We just wanted you to know we are leaving the church and starting our own church."

I was shocked.

"We just thought we should let you know," they said.

After I regained my composure, I said, "I have been your pastor and friend for a number of years. Don't you think we should have discussed something as important as starting a new church?"

"Oh, no, the Lord told us."

So I said, "Okay. Bye." That was it.

Their church lasted six months. People were hurt, discouraged, and scattered because of the hardness of their hearts toward God's direction. A true sign of a focused heart is openness to God and to people.

Vision for Your Future

Your vision, sense of purpose, and destiny are related to what you do, but they also have to do with your view of the future. Your vision is a big part of your inner health, peace, and joy. It is critical to gain God's perspective of the dreams, desires, and purposes in your heart.

As a rule, young people are happier than older people because they have a future ahead of them. Often older people feel like they have only the past. If you have difficulty finding peace and joy, maybe you are spending too much time looking back. What is your vision? What is your dream? What is your hope of tomorrow? Do you have a sense of destiny?

If your response is "I'm just trying to make a living and pay the bills," then what do you expect?

Perhaps you want way too little because you have a survival lifestyle. A dog survives with some food and water. The fish is happy with a couple of sprinkles. But you cannot be happy just surviving.

Remember, you are made in the likeness and image of God. You are designed with visions and dreams. Children are born with visions and dreams. From the time they get a little truck or ball, they say, "I'm going to be a fireman. I am going to be a policeman. I'm going to be in the NFL." You cannot tell them they cannot achieve their dreams, because their world is filled with a future of visions and dreams.

Unfortunately for some, after they hang around adults long enough, it's taken out of them. "Get real.

Get a job and make a living. You'll be lucky if you can buy a Chevy. Stop looking at those Mercedes."

I was sitting in the first-class section of an airplane, and this mother dragged her little girl in. Things had slowed while people put their bags in overhead compartments. They were standing in first class for a moment. The little girl looked at the first-class seats and said to her mother, "Let's sit in these seats." The mom grabbed the little girl and said, "Don't even think about it. We don't sit up here," then dragged her child to the coach section. You may believe that type of attitude is humble, but it is sad to see kids taught to think small, poor, and pessimistic.

Recently, I was with a rabbi from Seattle. He preached prosperity to me. He said, "The reason America is declining is a lack of visions and dreams for prosperity. People do not dream to have families that prosper and generations that are blessed, passing it on to the future. All they're thinking about is surviving and 'who is going to take care of me and give me Medicare and a pharmacy supply?'" A Jewish man believed God has a better plan for him because he read the Bible. We call it the Old Testament, but for him it is the only testament, and he has received more visions and dreams than many of us have.

As I mentioned previously, Proverbs 29:18 KJV says, "Where there is no vision, the people perish...." Many people do not have a prophetic view of the future, or even of tomorrow.

We lack restraint, or self-discipline, often because we have no purpose or vision for our future. Live your life with purpose, and then you will automatically be disciplined. Vision gives you a reason to press forward.

A young man does not want to take a shower, shave, or put on cologne until he meets a girl. Suddenly, he wakes up without an alarm clock, gets out a razor blade, and cleans up. He has a new vision.

Without vision, people perish. Without vision, marriages perish. When you first fell in love, you dreamed about the future: kids, a great house, travel, and doing things together.

After a few years into the marriage, you focus on packing lunches and getting the kids off to school. The vision is lost. You begin to say things like "I can't see us ever working it out and getting it together. My spouse is never going to change."

A lack of vision produces hopelessness. Vision is a positive view of the future, and hope is a positive view of something to come. When you have lost the vision for a good marriage, you have lost your hope. When you are hopeless, you soon feel helpless. You begin to say, "I've tried everything. Nothing I do makes a difference." When hopelessness and helplessness strike marriages, divorce lawyers start making money. Begin to talk again about the visions and dreams you once had for your marriage.

With a vision, we have hope. When we have hope, we feel strong. We know we can make a difference. We realize there is something we can do, and we're on our way to a glorious future.

There will be some mountains to climb, but we will shout when we get to the top. There will be some problems to solve, but the feeling of accomplishment will be worth the effort. We are going to have some challenges, but overcoming them will bring peace.

Visions, dreams, goals, challenges, and obstacles to overcome keep you strong, give you hope, and make you feel hopeful instead of helpless.

Jeremiah 29:11 NIV expresses God's thoughts about you:

> "For I know the plans I have for you," declares the Lord, "plans to prosper you and not to harm you, plans to give you hope and a future."

Set your mind on things above, not on things on the earth. God knows you better than you know yourself. If you focus on the things of God, you will prosper and experience success in every area of your life.

Questions

1. Where is your focus? In other words, what do you spend the most time thinking on (work, financial opportunities, difficulties in your family life, the Word of God)?

2. From which angle do you view your life—from God's perspective or the world's perspective of success?

3. What is the focus of your heart? Consider the three questions earlier in the chapter.

4. Write down three things in your life where you have struggled with opposing beliefs.

5. Have you violated your own conscience in the past? How did this affect your emotional and mental health?

9

※

Building Relationships With God and His People

In America today, many people think they are faithful if they make it to church once a month. In the natural, you eat more than once a month. Likewise, your spirit man is hungry for fellowship with God more than once a month. It takes daily and weekly commitment to build godly relationships.

A healthy heart desires to know God. If you do not know God, nothing else will make a lasting change in your life. You will just exchange one addiction for another, one problem for another.

> Blessed are those who keep His testimonies, who seek Him with the whole heart!
>
> Psalm 119:2

Many people are not looking to God at all. They are searching for a husband, a wife, a job, or money. God wants you to have a spouse. He wants you to have money and be blessed; but if you are not seeking Him, you cannot obtain any of these His way.

Christianity is not about what you get from God: "But seek ye first the kingdom of God, and his righteousness; and all these things shall be added unto you" (Matt. 6:33 KJV). It is about a relationship with Him.

You cannot get what God has for you if you don't want God. You cannot seek peace, joy, healing, prosperity, or happiness without seeking God. Those who seek Him are blessed. Do not just seek the gifts; seek the Giver.

Would you like it if your children said, "I want what Mom and Dad give me, but I don't want Mom and Dad in my life"? Would you think you had a problem with your family if your kids treated you with the attitude "Just give me what you have, but stay out of my life"? That is the way many of us treat God. "Heal me, bless me, touch me, make me happy, make me healthy, but then leave me alone; I'm watching TV."

There is so much new teaching that's available today. However, if it's not founded on a real relationship with God through the Lord Jesus Christ, it won't work.

We believe we can deal with the symptoms. We have convinced ourselves that if we just take the fat-burning pill, that will do it; that we do not have to change our mentality instead of our hearts, we do not have to change our habit, we do not have to change our lifestyle—we just need a pill. If you are having sex problems, just take a pill, and all of a sudden, "Here I am, Viagra® man." If you are depressed, just take a pill. If you have an attention deficit, just take a pill.

The attitude of the world is that everything can be dealt with from a symptom perspective. As we discussed in Chapter two, the characteristics of the orphaned heart require healing. If you do not like yourself, just change your nose. Cut off some stuff, pump up some stuff, or add some silicone. If you keep trying to deal with symptoms without changing the heart, what you do to yourself may actually make things worse.

God Looks at the Heart

We need to stop focusing on the symptoms and look at what matters to God: the heart. We see a great illustration of God looking at the heart in 1 Samuel 15.

Saul was king over Israel, but God got fed up with Saul. He told Saul in effect, "When you were small in your own eyes and served Me, I raised you up. Now you've lost your perspective on Who is important, so I'm taking the kingdom away from you." (1 Sam. 15:17-23.) God did not look for a new king based on people, polls, or the Democratic or Republican perspectives. God looked for a man after His own heart.

As we discussed earlier in the book, God found a little shepherd—a guitar-playing, praise-and-worship-singing leader named David—to replace Saul as king. Psalm 119:10 says, "With my whole heart I have sought You; Oh, let me not wander from Your commandments." Seeking God with a whole heart is the foundation for keeping a whole heart. Seek God with all that is within you. Desire to know God more than you want that new car or house.

If you love God with your whole heart, you cannot throw your Bible in the backseat of your car and not pick it up until the next time you show up at church. You have to decide to have a heart after God and take time to develop a relationship with Him.

God found that in David; God raised him up and made him the greatest leader Israel had ever known. Remember, the one thing David had going for him was he set his heart after God. If anything in the world is more important to you than a heart after God, then you are going to have to cry out, "God, help me get this thing turned around. I have been so wrapped up in materialism and in other wrong things. Help me to get my heart right so I can seek You with a whole heart."

In Matthew 5:8 Jesus says, "Blessed are the pure in heart, for they shall see God." The foundation of a healthy, whole heart is a desire for God—to know God, to walk with God, to have intimacy with God. When your heart is pure, whole, and right, in an open, close relationship with God, you will find the answer to the drug problem, the alcohol problem, the weight problem, the financial problem, and the marriage problem.

You must meet with God, go after Him, enter into His courts, sense His Presence, worship Him, talk to Him, hear from Him, and study His Word. When you desire God, He will give you everything.

Love God and People

Inner health requires intimacy with the Father and with His people. A whole heart includes intimate, open relationships with people who are going where you are going. Remember, God said you cannot love the Lord with all your heart without loving your neighbor as yourself. (Matt. 22:37-39.) You must have intimate relationships with people.

Someone said, "I love the Lord, but I hate people." The funny thing is that we are all made in His likeness and image. If you hate people, what are you really saying about God? You don't really love God; you love your fantasy.

Someone said, "I'm going to the mountains to get close to the Lord." If you want to get close to God, go to church. That is why God said, "Those who are planted in the house of the Lord shall flourish in the courts of our God" (Ps. 92:13). Relationships with those of like heart build us up and we grow stronger with God.

> If someone says, "I love God," and hates his brother, he is a liar; for he who does not love his brother whom he has seen, how can he love God whom he has not seen?
>
> 1 John 4:20

If you believe you love God but don't love people, don't want to serve, volunteer, or get involved, then you've deceived yourself. You can't love God, whom you haven't seen, if you don't love the people who surround you.

It's time to be honest with ourselves about relationships. Many times we do fine in situations where we can keep people at a distance, but a whole heart requires us to open up.

Proverbs 13:20 says, "He who walks with wise men will be wise, but the companion of fools will be destroyed." Make a decision to build positive, godly, intimate relationships.

From the Inside Out

The heart affects everything we do as Christians. As mentioned earlier, God works from the inside out, not from the outside in. You cannot deal with debt, sickness, relationship problems, or depression from an outward perspective. You must get to the heart. Out of your heart you will overcome all of the problems in your life.

If we view the keys to inner healing as vitamins, we soon realize we have daily minimum requirements in each of these areas. You need to have certain vitamins and minerals each day to be healthy. You cannot go for a year just eating junk and then eat carrots all day for one day. That will not make you healthy.

There is no reason why we can't live long, healthy lives if we eat a balanced diet and get the right vitamins. However, without the daily minimum requirements, we become malnourished. We struggle, we are tired, we are not feeling well, and we take medicine to cover up the symptoms. Many times the medicine is needed because we are not doing what is required for daily health.

Just as that is true in the natural realm, it is also true in the emotional and spiritual realms. If you will do what is necessary for daily minimum requirements, you will stay whole in your spirit, soul, and body.

A Call for Intimacy

Sincerely ask yourself, "Do I really want a relationship with God?" In reality, most of us do not. We just want healing, salvation, or blessing. We want a banker, a magician, someone to make us feel good. We want a doctor. But we do not want a relationship with God.

If worship is an expression of love and passion for God, it would be easy to come to the conclusion that many people do not want a relationship with God, because when it comes to worship, God is treated like a distant relative. Some treat God like a distant cousin who shows up on their Christmas card list.

Many leave God, the church, and their family because of a fear of intimacy. It's more comfortable to be into themselves and their own needs.

Many of us were reared in environments that were closed. My father was a very quiet person. He was a farm boy, reared in Nebraska. He only talked to the corn. Then he moved to be near his family. He became a carpenter and was alone in his shop for eight to ten hours a day.

He did not talk when he came home. He was present in body, but the house seemed empty. The intimacy was not there. There was no abuse, but the lack of communication and intimacy pushed my mother into divorce.

The week my father died, I talked to him on the telephone. "Hey, Dad, how are you doing?"

"Oh, good. Everything's good."

"Still working as a carpenter?" I asked.

"Yeah."

"What are you doing this weekend, Dad?"

"Oh, nothing."

It was the same thing he did every weekend. I said, "Why don't you come over? We'll have lunch together." He had not seen my children in a while. "We'll get together and spend some time with each other. I'll come to pick you up."

"Oh, no," he insisted. "I don't think I have time." Two days later, he went out to feed the horse, sat down by the stall, and died. My last conversation with him was "Sorry. No thanks. I don't have time."

There is a tremendous need for intimate, close, honest relationships. Intimacy produces inner healing. You cannot live a closed life and be healthy.

Many of us walk into environments surrounded by people and ask, "How are you today?" "Good to see you." "How is the family?" Then we walk out the same way we walked in, with no one touching us.

We worship God much the same way. "Praise the Lord. Hallelujah." We are into ourselves and think we are okay. One day we will sit down alone and die, to be discovered a few hours later.

Intimacy is contact and connection with God and His people. We cannot have one or the other. Some say, "I'm close to the Lord—just me and the Lord—but not to people. I don't enjoy being around people." They live in a fantasy. They do not really have a relationship with God. People are made in the likeness and image of God. If you love God, you will love people.

Remember, in Matthew 22:36 the disciples came to Jesus and said, "Teacher, which is the great commandment in the law?" In other words, what is the number one statement, the greatest message in the entire Bible?

Jesus said:

"'You shall love the Lord your God with all your heart, with all your soul, and with all your mind.'

"This is the first and great commandment.

"And the second is like it: 'You shall love your neighbor as yourself.'"

Matthew 22:37-39

Jesus was saying, "You can't achieve the first without the second. They are synonymous. One is impossible without the other. Love people around you as you love yourself."

If all Scripture were summed up in one statement, it would be "Love the Lord your God and love the people around you as you love yourself."

We go through our daily lives—to church, to the office, and home—to be isolated and separated. Yet we do not understand why we are not experiencing the fullness, the joy, the peace, the happiness, and all the Bible says life has to offer. We lower our expectations and give up our dreams. We accept far less than we really want to because we figure "that's all there is." It is a result of our own lack of intimacy.

The thing that fascinated people about Jesus was that He wanted to get close; He wanted to connect with people. He was not about robes, titles, laws, or sermons of eloquence. He was about *people,* and the people responded.

In Jesus' days of ministry, lepers were placed in leper colonies and isolated from the community. People with leprosy were considered unclean.

Jesus approached the "unclean" people and laid hands on them. The Bible says He healed all manner of sickness and disease. (Matt. 4:23.) He touched them. He demonstrated "The Father is near to you. He wants to touch you. He wants to put His hands on you and be close to you."

When the children ran to Jesus, the disciples dismissed them by saying, "Get these children out of here. Can't you see the Man of God is busy?" But Jesus said, "'Let the little children come to Me, and do not forbid them; for of such is the kingdom of heaven.' And He laid His hands on them [to bless them]..."[1] (Matt. 19:14,15).

Some people live in isolation and separation. When they get around people, they wear a sign on their forehead that says, "Don't touch me." They avoid opportunities to be close to people, using excuses like "I don't have time. I don't want to go to someone's house. I won't know anyone there." People isolate themselves and, for whatever reason, decide to stay in the emotional leper colony.

We often isolate ourselves from our own family. The wife says to her husband, "Honey, how are you doing?"

He replies, "Fine."

"How was your day?"

"Fine."

"Everything okay?"

"Yes."

"Want to do anything?"

"No."

"Anything you want to talk about?"

"No."

"Want to go somewhere?"

"Mmmm."

She might as well be talking to an ape. We have lived in the emotional leper colony so long that we are numb. The peace and joy of the Lord has disappeared.

Proverbs 18:1 says, "A man who isolates himself seeks his own desire; he rages against all wise judgment." When you isolate yourself, you become your own counselor and teacher and you tell yourself what to do. You ask the question and give the answer. You rage against wise judgment and lower your expectations.

In many American schools when kids cannot pass a test, the level of testing is lowered. What harm would come if they were challenged to lift their vision, if someone said, "You can do it"?

Fulfillment is sought in perverted ways because there is no peace or joy. There is no end to it because there is no fulfillment through perversion. The person who desires evil will never be satisfied.

You say, "The last time I opened up, I was really hurt." That happens, but don't let that experience shut you down for the rest of your life. Try again. Open your heart and begin to build a relationship and intimacy. You cannot be intimate with God without relationship with people.

When I am home, I can be closed like my father if I do not force myself to open up. I work on the house and talk to my motorcycle.

My father was a team roper when he was not a carpenter. When I was fifteen, one of his horses stepped out of a moving trailer and the horse was badly hurt. My father put that horse in the barn, put him in a sling, and nursed him every day for six months. I remember thinking at the time, *Dad loves that horse. He talks to the horse more than he talks to me. He shows more affection to the horse than he does to me.* Every night for months, my dad would apply ointment to the horse and work with him. In spite of his care, the horse died. Dad was devastated.

Maybe you talk to your computer, your lawn mower, tools, or sports page more than to your children. To avoid intimacy, you fall in love with intangible objects.

A man can remember the statistics of every quarterback in the NFL, but will forgot important dates with his wife.

My wife helps me open up when she says, "Let's share" or "Let's get close."

I'll say, "I don't know what to say. Help me."

My wife will say, "Here's what I've been thinking. How do you feel about that?" She helps me. It is not always easy, but who said successfully fulfilling God's will would be easy? Jesus said, "Enter by the narrow gate; for wide is the gate and broad is the way that leads to destruction, and there are many who go in by it. Because narrow is the gate and difficult is the way which leads to life, and there are few who find it" (Matt. 7:13,14).

Intimacy and passion are required in your relationship with your spouse. The quality and depth of your sexual union will be evident in your emotional relationship. The Scripture says, "He knew her." Your relationship with your partner in life started mentally and emotionally and became physical.

Some people avoid relationships because they can bring the greatest pain; but they also produce the greatest reward. It's sad to be ninety-five years old and stuck in a retirement home where no one visits you. When you are 105, you should have so much going on that you have to tell people, "I need to spend more time with God."

Lack of intimacy causes anxiety, loneliness, and emptiness. The only cure is to break through the shell and overcome those things that have closed you up, and then get close to people.

Jesus says in John 8:31-32, "'...If you abide in My word, you are My disciples indeed. And you shall know the truth, and the truth shall make you free.'"

The literal Greek says, "You will know the truth," and *truth* is defined in the Greek dictionary as "...not concealing...."[2] When nothing is concealed, you will be free. Jesus is dealing with the Word in the disciples. Let's apply it to our lives.

I know the truth because I am in relationship, I am open for counsel, and I receive wise judgment. I know the truth because I haven't concealed my life. I don't have secrets; my life is an open book. The truth will make me free.

Be honest with yourself. The reason we avoid relationships is not that we are shy. It is usually that there is something we do not want people to know about us.

What if I were the pastor at Christian Faith Center for twenty years and had never revealed that I had been in a drug rehabilitation program and had been in jail? "Oops, I just forgot to mention it." One day the local paper has a headline that reads, "Casey Treat, pastor of Christian Faith Center, was once involved in drugs and jailed." That would be hot news. The congregation would be very upset. "I can't believe it. I've been attending this church for years, and he never revealed that he once used drugs?" It would be news because I hid it.

Anything that is hidden is powerful, but there is no power to what is uncovered. Bondage comes from lying and hiding. Freedom comes from truth and openness. Openness and honesty allow us to be free and deal with the problems of life.

No one is born with the ability to be intimate, open, and honest. You have to fight your feelings and all that is normal in the world. You have to swim upstream. Any old dead fish can float downstream. You have to swim upstream. That takes effort.

By opening up with one another, intimacy begins to take place, which results in inner healing.

Questions

1. Have you seen changes in your relationships as you have learned to think and act according to God's Word?

2. What place in your life do you give relationships with mature Christians?

3. Examine your relationships and commitments. Do you have the relationships you want with God and with people?

4. Have you isolated yourself? Have you become your own counselor and teacher?

10

Being Led by the Spirit

Your life can be full, healthy, and whole when you rely on the Holy Spirit. Practice each step to a healthy, whole heart daily. In John 14:16 Jesus says, "And I will pray the Father, and He will give you another Helper, that He may abide with you forever." The *King James Version* calls the Holy Spirit "Comforter." The Holy Spirit is with you forever. Are you listening to Him? Daily take advantage of His Presence in your life.

How many times have you done things and later thought, *Why did I do that?* While you were doing it, your spirit was saying, "Don't do this." You did it anyway because of your anger, frustration, fear, or flesh, and afterwards that still, small voice was still saying, "I told you, don't do that." The Holy Spirit abides with you forever, and if you follow Him, obey Him, and listen to Him, you will receive the benefits—ingredients for a successful life.

Jesus continues to describe the Holy Spirit and His role in our lives in John 14:17-18:

> "the Spirit of truth; whom the world cannot receive, because it neither sees Him nor knows Him; but you know Him, for He dwells with you and will be in you.
>
> "I will not leave you orphans; I will come to you."

The Comforter, the Helper, the Holy Spirit, is going to teach and show you how to think and live to avoid the characteristics of an orphaned heart. You will not be insecure, inferior, or defensive. You will not get puffed up trying to prove you are someone, nor will you get scared and hide because you think you are no one. With the help of the Holy Spirit, you will be able to walk in truth.

In John 14:26 Jesus says, "But the Helper, the Holy Spirit, whom the Father will send in My name, He will teach you all things...." Notice it says, "...He will teach you *all* things...." You may say, "I don't know what to do in this relationship." If you are walking in the Spirit, you will know. If you are listening to and being led by the Spirit, "He will teach you all things."

A wife might say, "I can't understand this man. He is driving me crazy. No matter what I do, I cannot please him. I don't know what's going on. His head is so thick, it's like a brick." The reason you talk like that is that you are in your flesh. If you respond by asking the Spirit, He will teach you how to reach that man. He will teach you how to be the kind of wife who sanctifies her husband. Scripture says the wife can win her husband by her conduct, without a word. (1 Pet. 3:1.)

A dad might say, "How do I handle these teenagers?" The Holy Spirit knows what's going on with them. If we as parents will walk in the Spirit, He will teach us how to talk, build, and lead, rather than control our teens.

This is why we need a relationship with the Holy Spirit. This is why we want to stay in the Spirit: so that everything that is in the kingdom can be manifested in our lives.

Many times we start out well believing God, but we give up too soon. We fall just about the time the promise is ready to manifest. You can do the right thing for weeks, then quit and miss the blessing; but your efforts will produce if you stay the course.

A healthy heart endures. Hebrews 10:36 says, "For you have need of endurance [or patience], so that after you have done the will of God, you may receive the promise."

You cannot lead the marathon for 26 miles. You have to lead for 26.2 miles. You cannot lead the game for eight innings. You have to be in the lead at the bottom of the ninth. "But let patience have her perfect work, that ye may be perfect and entire, wanting nothing" (James 1:4 KJV).

Someone once asked me, "What's the one thing you've done to have a good relationship with your kids?"

I said, "There's no *one thing*. You cannot bake a cake with one ingredient. You cannot raise a family with one thing. It is a bunch of things, and you've got to do them consistently year after year."

It has been said, "If you are willing to believe forever, it will only take a moment." If you are willing to stand for what you are believing for, then your faith is strong and God will be faithful to bring results to your faith sooner than you think.

I heard about a young singer who was supposedly an overnight success. She sold a zillion records at twenty years of age. However, she had begun dancing lessons at four years of age. She had been on the stage singing at five years of age. She had been performing for fifteen years. Finally, at twenty, she was beginning to see success. She endured.

Patience produces good fruit and a long, successful life. You can't have a successful life by human effort or by your own mind, energy, and work. When you are led by God's Spirit, you have an increased ability to endure, and then you succeed.

As we draw near to God, He draws near to us. As we open our lives, He fills us. Without the Holy Spirit, we can be dedicated and work hard but eventually give up. Many people are in this state. They have more self-help books than they know what to do with.

Walk in the Spirit

Living a Spirit-directed life begins with developing a relationship with the Holy Spirit.

Galatians 5:16 says, "…Walk in the Spirit, and you shall not fulfill the lust of the flesh." When we choose to listen to the Spirit of God, then all that is in the kingdom works for us.

There are just three steps that will bring you into a Spirit-directed life. First, you must be born of the Spirit of God. Second, you must be filled with the Spirit, and third, you must make a decision to follow the direction of the Spirit.

Be Born Again

In John 3, Nicodemus approaches Jesus and wants to know how to be born again:

There was a man of the Pharisees named Nicodemus, a ruler of the Jews.

This man came to Jesus by night and said to Him, "Rabbi, we know that You are a teacher come from God; for no one can do these signs that You do unless God is with him."

182

Jesus answered and said to him, "Most assuredly, I say to you, unless one is born again, he cannot see the kingdom of God."

John 3:1-3

Jesus did not talk this way to the average guy on the street, but Nicodemus was a religious man, a ruler of the Jews, who acted as if he knew everything.

The Lord simply said, in essence, "If you don't get born again, you have nothing. You can talk spiritually, but if you are not born again, there is no life in you. Unless you are born again, you'll never see the kingdom of God. You will have no life in you, Nicodemus."

Nicodemus said to Him, "How can a man be born when he is old? Can he enter a second time into his mother's womb and be born?"

Jesus answered, "Most assuredly, I say to you, unless one is born of water and the Spirit, he cannot enter the kingdom of God."

John 3:4,5

"Born of water" refers to physical birth. The second birth is of the Spirit. "That which is born of the flesh is flesh, and that which is born of the Spirit is spirit" (John 3:6).

Notice the first word "Spirit" is capitalized, but the second word "spirit" is not. We could read it like this: "Your flesh is born of water, but your spirit must be born of the Spirit." The Holy Spirit will cause your human spirit to come alive. The new birth is all about an awakening of your spirit being.

First Corinthians 6:17 says, "But he who is joined to the Lord is one spirit with Him." If you believe in Jesus and He is your Lord and Savior, then you are joined to Him by faith.

A Christian's focus should not be to cause his spirit to become stronger but to cause his mind and emotions to step out of the way so his spirit can lead his life. As believers, we are one in the Spirit with Christ.

Our spirit and the Holy Spirit are made one. If you choose your own way of thinking and doing things, then your flesh will run your life. Although your spirit is one with God, it can be pushed aside. It becomes dormant while your mind and flesh control your life. The kingdom is never manifested in you. You have this vast relationship and all that the kingdom has to offer, but if you are not tapped into the Holy Spirit, your fears, emotions, attitudes, and anger rule.

Let's walk in the Spirit. The righteousness, peace, and joy of the kingdom are in the Spirit. Let's set our mind in agreement with our spirit: "I refuse to do what anger tells me to do. I will not do what fear tells me to do. I will not obey my past. I choose to do what the Spirit of God tells me to do. When I walk in the Spirit, everything that the kingdom has comes to me." You can be saved, but if you are not in the Spirit, you can miss what the kingdom has for you.

Many people have shoved the Spirit into a small corner of their lives. We look to make sure He's there on Sunday mornings, but the rest of the week we follow our mind, our will, and the world. Then we wonder, *Where is the peace and joy?*

The peace and joy of the kingdom that is lasting are only available in the Holy Spirit. When you talk to your wife, are you listening to your spirit or your flesh—your anger, frustration, anxiety, and selfishness?

If you are in the Spirit, you will have patience and all the benefits from God. Walking in the Spirit is a lifestyle. When you become plugged into the Spirit, there will be more spiritual desire and ability.

You will not get it all in one day. You have to walk in it. You have to live and practice it. It starts with being born again. When you are born of the Spirit, then you can be taught by the Spirit, led by the Spirit, and comforted by the Spirit.

The Holy Spirit will teach you all things. He will bring to your remembrance the things the Lord has spoken to you. Maybe you feel you cannot remember Scripture very well. If you are listening to the Holy Spirit, then He will remind you of Scriptures. He will give you biblical principles for the decisions that you are facing. When you are born of the Spirit, you can be taught, directed, and comforted by the Spirit.

Still, you must be willing to grow. In John 16:13 Jesus says, "When He, the Spirit of truth, has come, He will guide you into all truth; for He will not speak on His own authority, but whatever He hears He will speak; and He will tell you things to come." I know some investors who wish they had listened to the Holy Spirit and gotten out of the market the day before it crashed. Listen, and He will guide you. God will lead you through any challenge.

Be Filled With the Spirit

The second step you need to take to live a Spirit-directed life is to be filled with the Spirit. There is a difference between being born of the Spirit and being filled with the Spirit. Some of us have come up with our own definitions and explanations based on religion. We say, "I have my own way of relating with the Lord." You cannot do things your way. You must do things His way.

Someone said, "I know I have the Holy Spirit because I felt glory balls bursting over my head and hot oil coming down on me. I know that was the Lord." Well, I felt that when I saw my wife for the first time.

"I know the Lord was there because I felt goose bumps." I felt goose bumps the first time I went to a Rolling Stones concert.

I am not going to base my doctrine and my relationship with the Lord on a feeling. We must go to the Word of God. Feelings and our own perspectives may be right, or they may be wrong. We must go to the Word and discover what God says, because His Word is the solid rock on which we stand. This is where we build our foundation. Heaven and earth will pass away; glory balls, hot oil, and goose bumps will pass away, but the Word of God will never pass away. It will never change.

You Decide

You are faced with a choice. Are you going to be born of the Spirit and filled with the Spirit, or are you going to try to get through life on your own? Remember what Jesus said. You can say what you want about the Son of God, but when you blaspheme the Holy Spirit, you are in a heap of trouble. (Mark 3:29.)

Acts 19 says that Paul came to Ephesus and found some disciples. This is what happened:

> He said to them, "Did you receive the Holy Spirit when you believed?" So they said to him, "We have not so much as heard whether there is a Holy Spirit."
>
> And he said to them, "Into what then were you baptized?" So they said, "Into John's baptism."
>
> Acts 19:2,3

In other words, they repented and believed in the Messiah, but they did not understand the Holy Spirit. Paul recognized that they were disciples but weren't filled with the Spirit, so he asked the question, "Did you receive the Holy Spirit?"

I think Paul would ask the same question in many churches today. About halfway through the service he'd say, "Pastor, may I ask a question? I see you are all disciples, and you love the Lord, but have you received the Holy Spirit?"

Many churches would say, "We don't believe in that anymore." Can you imagine the man who wrote two-thirds of the New Testament coming to many of our churches today and not being allowed to preach what he wrote because we do not want the Holy Spirit?

> And when Paul had laid his hands on them, the Holy Spirit came upon them, and they spoke with tongues and prophesied.
>
> Acts 19:6

If Paul walked into your house today and recognized that you were a disciple but the Spirit of God was not in your life, he would ask, "Have you received the Holy Spirit?"

You might say, "I heard about it. Once I felt a glory ball and a goose bump."

I believe Paul would say, "Let me lay my hands on you, and let's pray and ask God to fill you with the Holy Spirit, and you will start speaking in other tongues."

The gospel has not changed. We cannot start throwing out Scriptures and say they passed away. We say we believe the Bible and trust this Book for our eternal salvation. It is time to be filled with the Holy Spirit and pray with other tongues.

I'm not sure which is worse: to say we don't even believe in the Holy Spirit, or to say we believe in Him but don't want to talk about Him publicly. That is compromising Christianity. We are not shouting in tongues, rolling on the floor, and acting crazy. We should never be embarrassed about, grieve, or quench the Spirit of God.

I will never forget the twelve-year-old daughter of one of our Bible school teachers. She attended a Baptist Bible camp, where they did not pray in the Spirit and did not believe in the work of the Holy Spirit. At camp each evening, she showed the little kids Scriptures about the Holy Spirit and prayed for them. She was getting all the kids at the camp filled with the Holy Spirit.

When the camp pastor found out, he called the little girl in. He told the little girl, "You need to stop talking about this stuff, because we don't believe in the Holy Spirit. That passed away, and it doesn't work anymore."

The little girl looked that pastor right in the eyes and asked, "Have you received the Holy Spirit since you believed?" God's Word in the mouth of a twelve-year-old is just as powerful as God's Word in anyone's mouth. That little girl may have changed that pastor's life.

The last words Jesus uttered before He ascended into heaven were very important. "And He said to them, 'Go into all the world and preach the gospel to every creature. He who believes and is baptized will be saved; but he who does not believe will be condemned'" (Mark 16:15,16).

That is the Great Commission. It is for every believer. We must embrace the call to go into all the world and preach the gospel to everyone, recognizing that those who believe and are baptized are going to be saved, but those who do not believe are going to hell forever.

Do you care if your brother spends eternity in hell? Do you care if anyone spends eternity separated from God? In Mark 16:17 Jesus says, "And these signs will follow those who believe...." If you believe, there will be evidence.

Many Christians are always looking for signs to follow. That is backwards. Christians are not to follow signs. We are to follow the Holy Spirit. As Christians, we are to follow the Holy Spirit and signs will follow us.

"...In My name they will cast out demons..." (Mark 16:17). If demons show up, cast them out. I am not afraid of Satan. Send one twelve-year-old believer. Cast that demon out in the name of Jesus. No holy water and wooden crosses are needed. Let's do away with religious Christianity and bring some believers on the scene.

"...they will speak with new tongues" (Mark 16:17). Do you speak with new tongues? Speaking with new tongues is the evidence of the Holy Spirit's baptism. Jesus said it.

We need people who are full of the Holy Spirit. We need some businesspeople praying in other tongues. We need moms and dads praying.

In Mark 16:18 Jesus continues with signs that will follow believers: "they will take up serpents; and if they drink anything deadly, it will by no means hurt them; they will lay hands on the sick, and they will recover."

He did not say, "Go out and find a snake and pick it up to prove that you're a Christian." That is silly. We are not going to go out and find serpents to prove anything. He was saying, "If you are ministering and doing My work and a serpent happens to bite you, you will overcome the deadly effects of it. If someone tries to poison you, you will overcome it." No one and no poison can stop you if you are working in the name of the Lord.

First, we must be born of the Spirit; then we must be filled with the Spirit. Then there will be evidence of the power of the Holy Spirit in our lives.

Wait for the Promise

Before Jesus ascended, He said, "Don't go anywhere, don't leave Jerusalem, until you receive what I am talking about, the Holy Spirit." Acts 1:4 says, "And being assembled together with them, He commanded them not to depart from Jerusalem, but to wait for the Promise of the Father...." They were already born again. John 20:22 says, "...He breathed on them, and said to them, 'Receive the Holy Spirit.'" So they were born of the Spirit, but they had to be filled with the Spirit. Jesus said, "Don't leave until you have received the Holy Spirit." That was the Promise of the Father.

> "For John truly baptized with water, but you shall be baptized with the Holy Spirit not many days from now.
>
> "But you shall receive power when the Holy Spirit has come upon you; and you shall be witnesses to Me in Jerusalem, and in all Judea and Samaria, and to the end of the earth."
>
> Acts 1:5,8

Acts 2:1-4 tells us about the infilling (or the baptism) of the Holy Spirit on the Day of Pentecost:

> Now when the Day of Pentecost had fully come, they were all with one accord in one place.
>
> And suddenly there came a sound from heaven, as of a rushing mighty wind, and it filled the whole house where they were sitting.

Then there appeared to them divided tongues, as of fire, and one sat upon each of them.

And they were all filled with the Holy Spirit and began to speak with other tongues, as the Spirit gave them utterance.

Mary, the mother of Jesus, spoke in tongues. Peter, James, and John prayed in other tongues. All of the 120 in the Upper Room prayed in other tongues, and it began to flow out of that room. The first thing Peter preached was "The Holy Spirit is going to give you visions and dreams when you repent and receive the gift of the Holy Spirit." (v. 17.)

In Acts 10:44-47 the Gentiles also received the baptism of the Holy Spirit:

While Peter was still speaking these words, the Holy Spirit fell upon all those who heard the word.

And those of the circumcision who believed were astonished, as many as came with Peter, because the gift of the Holy Spirit had been poured out on the Gentiles also.

Acts 10:44,45

The Spirit was poured out on the Gentiles. "For they heard them speak with tongues and magnify God.

Then Peter answered, 'Can anyone forbid water, that these should not be baptized who have received the Holy Spirit just as we have?'" (Acts 10:46,47).

This was up to eight years after the Day of Pentecost, and they were still being baptized with the Holy Spirit and praying with other tongues. When did it stop? When we got religious. When we went into the Dark Ages. When we wanted religion instead of the Lord. When we did not have the Word in our own language. When we followed man instead of Scripture. Nevertheless, God has brought it back for these last days.

"And it shall come to pass in the last days, says God, that I will pour out of My Spirit on all flesh...."

Acts 2:17

When we are filled with the Holy Spirit, we receive power and begin to pray in other tongues, just as the New Testament says. When we are born of the Spirit and filled with the Spirit, we can walk in the Spirit and all of the kingdom benefits—such as righteousness, peace, joy, healing, wholeness, prosperity, and protection—are ours. Everything the kingdom has to offer starts flowing into our lives.

Don't miss God's benefits in this life. Jesus did not say, "Wait till you get to heaven." He said to pray, "Your kingdom come. Your will be done on earth as it is in heaven" (Matt. 6:10). Let's inject a little bit of heaven in our lives now.

If we spend a little time praying in the Holy Spirit over our spouse, there will be good results in our marriage. If we spend time praying in the Spirit with our children, we will see change, healing, and blessings. If we will pray in the Holy Spirit before going into business negotiations, we will have breakthroughs. The Lord will guide us. Plug into the Spirit.

Ephesians 5:18 in *The Amplified Bible* says, "…but ever be filled and stimulated with the [Holy] Spirit." The Greek text literally says, "Be intoxicated with the Holy Spirit."[1] Do not get drunk with the wine of the world, but get intoxicated with the Spirit of God.

Look for peace, joy, comfort, excitement, and all the things you desire in the Holy Spirit. You are going to get them from the Holy Spirit. Acts 4:31 AMP says:

> And when they had prayed, the place in which they were assembled was shaken; and they were all

filled with the Holy Spirit, and they continued to speak the Word of God with freedom and boldness and courage.

Wait a minute. They were filled back in Acts 2. Why are they getting filled again in Acts 4 when they have already been filled? This is not a one-time deal. "*Ever be filled* with the Holy Spirit" (as we saw in Eph. 5:18) means it is a lifestyle. Stay filled with the Holy Spirit.

I do not mean that you will lose part of the Spirit. I just mean that you are to stay plugged in, remain alert, and be involved.

If we will stay plugged in and remain sensitive to the Holy Spirit, all that the kingdom of God has to offer will manifest in our lives. He will empower us, lead and guide us, and bring us into all the Father has promised.

Questions

1. What dreams have you given up?

2. What things are you willing to overcome to accomplish or receive your visions and dreams?

3. Are you taking advantage of the Holy Spirit's Presence in your life?

4. Are you taking time to receive wisdom and understanding for your family, business, and other areas of your life?

Conclusion

I hope this book has allowed you to discover the condition of your own heart. Once you *become aware,* you can *renew your mind* daily by replacing negative thoughts with what the Word of God says about you. Realize you have the ability to choose what goes into your heart, therefore controlling what comes out if it. *Protect* your heart by continually removing things that should not grow there. *Confess* what is wrong in your heart and what is right, God's Word. *Focus* and gain God's perspective of your life, and develop a deeper relationship with God and His people. Finally, *practice* these steps and apply them to your life with the help of the Holy Spirit.

I pray that you have received direction that will help you be a stronger, happier, and more effective Christian. I prayerfully agree with you to overcome the limitations that may hinder your life and to rise to the full measure of Christ so you may fulfill His will for your life and destiny.

Pray this prayer and begin to experience the new you—with a healed, whole heart.

Father, help me to be aware of my heart's condition and to be honest with myself; to make right choices; to confess, not only my sins but my pains, problems, and challenges, to strong Christians who will pray and agree with Your Word; to focus my thoughts on You and Your thoughts; to develop intimate, open, and lasting relationships; to protect my heart and be selective about its input. And, Lord, help me to endure and persevere until I see a manifestation of Your promises in my life, in Jesus' name. Amen.

Endnotes

Chapter 2

[1] M. Scott Peck, M.D., *The Road Less Traveled: A New Psychology of Love, Traditional Values and Spiritual Growth* (New York: Touchstone, Simon & Schuster, 1998).

[2] Based on a definition from *American Dictionary of the English Language,* 10th ed. (San Francisco: Foundation for American Christian Education, 1998). Facsimile of Noah Webster's 1828 edition, permission to reprint by G. & C. Merriam Company, copyright 1967 & 1995 (Renewal) by Rosalie J. Slater, s.v. "DISCIPLE."

Chapter 4

[1] Thayer and Smith, *The KJV New Testament Greek Lexicon,* "Greek Lexicon entry for Pikria," <http://www.biblestudy tools.net/Lexicons/Greek/grk.cgi?number=4088&version=kjv>.

[2] James Strong, *Strong's Exhaustive Concordance of the Bible,* "Greek Dictionary of the New Testament" (Nashville: Abingdon, 1890), p. 77, entry #5453, s.v. "springing," Hebrews 12:15.

[3] Ibid, p. 48, entry #3392, s.v. "be defiled," Hebrews 12:15.

Chapter 6

[1] "...this is the *fruit,* a Christian temper and disposition, a Christian life and conversation, Christian devotions and Christian designs. We must honour God, and do good, and exemplify the purity and power of the religion we profess; and this is bearing fruit...." Matthew Henry, *Matthew Henry Complete Commentary on the Whole Bible,* "Commentary on John 15," <http://bible.crosswalk.com/

Commentaries/MatthewHenryComplete/mhc-com.cgi?book=
joh&chapter=015>.

2 ...As the vinedresser will remove all branches that are dead or that
bear no fruit, so will God take from his church all professed
Christians who give no evidence by their lives that they are truly
united to the Lord Jesus. He here refers to such cases as that of Judas,
the apostatizing disciples, and all false and merely nominal
Christians...." *Barnes' Notes,* by Albert Barnes, D.D., Electronic
Database (Biblesoft, copyright © 1997). All rights reserved. See
"John 15:2."

3 Based on Thayer and Smith, "Greek Lexicon entry for Katharos"
<http://www.bible studytools.net/Lexicons/Greek/studytools.net/
Lexicons/Greek/grk.cgi?number=2513&version=kjv>, and "Greek
Lexicon entry for Kathairo," http://www.biblestudytools.net/
Lexicons/Greek/grk.cgi?number=2508&version=kjv>.

Chapter 7

1 "It is not necessary to assume that Paul had never been married.
Marriage was regarded as a duty among the Jews so that a man was
considered to have sinned if he had reached the age of twenty
without marrying...A rabbinical precept declared that a Jew who has
no wife is not a man. It is not certain, but most probable, that Saul
[who later became Paul] was a member of the Sanhedrin (Acts
26:10). If so, he must have been married, as marriage was a condition of membership. From 1 Corinthians 7:8 it is plausibly inferred
that he classed himself among widowers." *Vincent's Word Studies of
the New Testament,* Electronic Database (Biblesoft, copyright ©
1997). All rights reserved. See "1 Corinthians 7:7."

2 Based on a definition from *Webster's II New College Dictionary*
(Boston/New York: Houghton Mifflin Company, 1995), s.v. "rebuke."

[3] "…It is now estimated that a talent was equal to approximately one thousand dollars…." Spiros Zodhiates Th.D., *The Complete Word Study Dictionary New Testament* (Chattanooga, Tennessee: AMG Publishers, 1993) p. 1365, entry #5007, s.v. "talent," Matthew 18:24.

Chapter 9

[1] Matthew Henry, "Commentary on Matthew 19," <http://bible.cross walk.com/Commentaries/MatthewHenryComplete/mhc-com.cgi?book=mt&chapter=019>. See "Verses 13-15."

[2] James Strong, *Strong's Exhaustive Concordance, Compact Edition,* "Greek Dictionary of the New Testament" (Nashville: Broadman Press, 1983), p. 9, entry #227, s.v. "truth," John 8:32.

Chapter 10

[1] Ibid, p. 47, entry #3184, s.v. "drunk," Ephesians 5:18.

Prayer of Salvation

A born-again, committed relationship with God is the key to the victorious life. Jesus laid down His life and rose again so that we could spend eternity with Him in heaven and experience His absolute best on earth. If you would like to receive Jesus into your life in order to become born again, pray this prayer from your heart:

Heavenly Father, I come to You admitting that I am a sinner. Right now, I choose to turn away from sin, and I ask You to cleanse me of all unrighteousness. I believe that Your Son Jesus died on the cross to take away my sins. I also believe that He rose again from the dead so that I might be justified and made righteous through faith in Him. I call upon the name of Jesus Christ to be the Savior and Lord of my life. Jesus, I choose to follow You, and I ask that You fill me with the power of the Holy Spirit. I declare that right now I am a child of God. I am free from sin and am full of the righteousness of God. I am saved in Jesus' name. Amen.

If you have prayed this prayer to receive Jesus Christ as your Savior, or if this book has changed your life, we would like to hear from you. Please write us at:

Harrison House Publishers
P.O. Box 35035
Tulsa, Oklahoma 74153

You can also visit us on the Web at
www.harrisonhouse.com

About the Author

Casey Treat is the senior pastor of Christian Faith Center in Seattle, Washington, and ministers to over 6000 people weekly. He is an author, teacher, and motivational speaker. His television program, *Living On Course,* is currently seen worldwide.

Casey Treat was born and reared in a suburb of Seattle, Washington. As a teenager, he was heavily involved with drugs and entered the former Washington Drug Rehabilitation Center, a Christian-based program founded by Julius Young. It was there that Casey was born again, called into ministry, and began to develop his leadership philosophies.

Casey entered Bible college, where he met and, in 1978, married Wendy Peterson. They served in their local church, conducted Bible study groups, and toured the Seattle area with their musical group, The New Version. Casey also started a local radio broadcast and worked as the Associate Director of Washington Drug Rehabilitation Center.

In their last two years of Bible College, Casey and Wendy began to sense the call of God on their lives to plant a church. On January 6, 1980, Casey and Wendy founded Christian Faith Center and began to pastor a group of thirty. They were ordained in July 1980 by Dr. Fred Price at Crenshaw Christian Center in Los Angeles, California.

In 1984, Casey and Wendy founded cfs.asp Christian Faith School for preschoolers through twelfth graders, and later Dominion College.

With the first annual vision.asp Vision International Leadership Conference in 1985, Casey and Wendy launched ministers.asp Vision Ministers Fellowship. This organization provides support for men and women in leadership who want to grow and more fully develop themselves and their ministries through teaching, mentoring, and relationship building. Casey and Wendy Treat have been instrumental in helping to plant and support numerous churches through this ministry.

Casey and Wendy Treat and their three children reside in the Seattle area.

To contact Casey Treat,
please write:

Casey Treat
Christian Faith International
P.O. Box 98800
Seattle, WA 98198

www.caseytreat.com

*Please include your prayer requests
and comments when you write.*

Also From Harrison House
by Casey Treat

Renewing the Mind: The Foundation of Your Success

Other Books by Casey Treat

Fulfilling Your God Given Destiny

Love, Sex and Kids

You Can Pull Down Strongholds and Break Old Habits

Leadership Matrix

Additional copies of this book
are available from your local bookstore.

HARRISON HOUSE

Tulsa, Oklahoma 74153

The Harrison House Vision

Proclaiming the truth and the power

Of the Gospel of Jesus Christ

With excellence;

Challenging Christians to

Live victoriously,

Grow spiritually,

Know God intimately.